# Cheerful Memories / Troubled Years

Aba, Misha and Ida Taratuta
*New York, 2010*

Library of Congress Cataloging-in-Publication Data

Names: Taratuta, Aba, author. | Taratuta, Ida, author.
Title: Cheerful memories/troubled years : a story of a refusenik's family
  in Leningrad and its struggle for immigration to Israel / Aba and Ida Taratuta.
Description: Boston : Cherry Orchard Books, an imprint of Academic Studies
  Press, 2019. | Includes index.
Identifiers: LCCN 2019007840 (print) | LCCN 2019008826 (ebook) |
  ISBN 9781644690451 | ISBN 9781644690437 (hardcover) |
  ISBN 9781644690444 (pbk.)
Subjects: LCSH: Taratuta, Aba—Family. | Refuseniks. |
  Jews—Persecutions—Soviet Union. | Jews—Soviet Union—Migrations. |
  Soviet Union—Emigration and immigration—Government policy. | Soviet
  Union—Ethnic relations. | Israel—Emigration and immigration
Classification: LCC DS134.93.T37 (ebook) | LCC DS134.93.T37 A3 2019 (print) |
  DDC 323.1192/4047210922 [B] —dc23
LC record available at https://lccn.loc.gov/2019007840

Editors: Michael Beizer and Tamara Brill

This publication is supported by the Association "Remember and Save," Israel
11 Haprahim St., Apt 69, Haifa, 3473306, Israel
Tel: 972-4-8256959 or 972-5444-82569
aba.taratuta@gmail.com
Soviet-jews-exodus.com

On the cover: "Aliya shelanu" by Eugene Abeshaus, 1975.
Cover design by Ivan Grave.

Cherry
Orchard
Books

# Cheerful Memories / Troubled Years

A Story of a Refusenik's Family in Leningrad
and its Struggle for Immigration to Israel

Aba and Ida
TARATUTA

Boston
2019

Our very special thanks are extended to:
    **Stefani Hoffman, Enid Wurtman**, Israel,
    for editing the book,

A special thank you to:
    **Lena Romanovsky**, Israel,
    for the Russian-English translation.

**Edward Markov**, Israel,
    for development of photographic materials
    and for valuable advice in preparing the book,

**Igor Uspensky,** Israel,
    for valuable advice in editing the book.

Sincere gratitude to:
    **Alex Geller**,
    **Leonid Lotvin**,
    **Boris Ruchkan**,
    **Nina Simanovsky**,
    **Ilya Simovsky**,
    **Pavel Tsimberov**,
    all USA,
    for the Russian-English translation.

Special thanks to
    **Leonid Fridkin**, Israel,
    **Edward Markov**, Israel,
    **Yael Pushkin**, Israel,
    **Natan Rodzin**, USA,
    **Lena Yeroshina**, Russia,
    **Tamara Kazakevich**, USA,
    for permission to use their material.

Dedicated to our grandchildren
*Daniel Jacob* and *Benjamin Simon Taratuta*

# Contents

# From the Editor

This book was conceived as a family history written for the grandchildren. Hence, the authors' personal approach and the significance of their family history. However, the text includes only a small part of the pedigree of the family Taratuta, as written by an Israeli cousin, and should not outweigh the primary author's text. Ida Taratuta is listed as the co-author because she wrote the first chapter, and because, together with her husband, she reconstructed the events and facts of the entire experience.

In the process of working on the book, the authors, in addition to depending on their memories, used a three-page diary with a list of the main events of their life in refusal for 1973–88 (the reader will find a facsimile in the attachments), and the record of Aba's interrogation by the KGB in 1982, which he wrote immediately upon returning home. Taratuta managed to get these four pages out of the USSR. Dozens of unique, first published, carefully attributed photos give this edition a special value.

Memories differ. Having known the author, my friend and senior colleague in the struggle, for thirty-five years, and being familiar with the events described both as a participant and as an historian, I can confidently say that we have in him a credible witness who writes concisely with a clear mind and memory, sometimes with humor, but without dramatizing the events or boasting. You yourself will see this after reading the book.

*Dr. Michael Beizer*
*The Hebrew University of Jerusalem*
*November 2015*

# From the Authors

Dear grandchildren, Dan and Ben,

You live in the United States, far from our Israel, and farther still from Russia, the country where we were born and raised. When you become fathers and grandfathers, you may want to learn more about the history of your family and about how we lived; then you will need this book with its brief and entertaining story about our experiences.

As you know, in the past, Russia, together with a number of other, now independent countries, was called the Soviet Union, whose citizens were not entitled to the rights and liberties common to Western countries. Particularly lacking was the right to leave one's own country. Soviet Jews who, in addition to enduring the general lawlessness, also suffered from state antisemitism, sought the right to immigrate to Israel. The state permitted some of them to emigrate, but it did not permit others to leave. These people were called "refuseniks."

"Refuseniks" faced a fateful choice: to wait submissively for the state to have mercy and release them from its grasp or to enter into an active struggle for repatriation and for the awakening of the Jewish identity of their compatriots. This could lead to not obtaining exit visas or even to imprisonment. We, your grandparents, chose the path of struggle for our rights and fought for them for fifteen years. This fight was the most important experience and the "finest hour" of our lives. In this book, we aim to tell you about our family history and about our involvement in the fight for Soviet Jewry. We hope it will interest both of you and anyone else who may be interested in Jewish activities in the 1970s and 1980s in the USSR.

*Grandmother Ida and Grandfather Aba*
*Haifa, 2012*

# 1.

# Grandmother Ida

## *My family*

My grandparents on my mother's side lived in Ukraine up to the 1917 Bolshevik Revolution, in the town of Krivoy Rog. Grandfather's name was Moses Nemirovsky and grandmother's, Cecilia Vodovoz. Grandfather's roots were probably from the Ukrainian city of Nemirov, as names often reflected the geography of the Pale of Settlement (and sometimes an individual's occupation). The family was not religious but observed Jewish traditions. Mother, who was born in 1902, was the only child of the family. At that time, a single child family was considered a rarity. The "official" rabbi registered her as Sonya. "Official rabbi" means that he was appointed by town officials and not by the Jewish community.

Grandfather owned a bakery where bread was baked for the miners who made up the bulk of the population of the city. They lived quite happily and owned a one-story stone house in the town. When the Bolsheviks came to power, they took away both the bakery and the house. Many years later, when we were in refusal, we went there with our friends, the Abeshauses. While boating by canoe in Ukraine, we arrived in Krivoy Rog. We decided to find this house, basing our search on mother's description. It was a one-story house with a high first floor and two entrances, but it did not look as big as mother had described....

During the Civil War, when the Bolsheviks tried to impose their power over the country, Krivoy Rog repeatedly passed from one opposing group to another; each change of power was accompanied by pogroms against the Jewish population. When the Bolsheviks finally established themselves in the town, they abolished the Pale of Settlement. At that time, the family moved to Moscow. Mother had turned twenty years old or so by the time of their move. She enrolled in medical school but was expelled as a daughter of *lishenets* (in the first years of Soviet power, "lishenets" referred to those who, before the Revolution, had owned property and were therefore deprived of many civil rights. The same rule applied to those who owned a small business or shop, in the years 1921–1929, when it was permitted by the so-called New Economic Policy, or NEP). My mother therefore graduated from secretarial courses and for many years, she worked as a typist, including during World War II. In addition, she was unusually talented in embroidery work as well as knitting and crocheting. As a result, she could also fill the most important orders for the workshops of women's clothing. Her "side income" thus substantially complemented our family budget.

My mother met her future husband in Moscow; his name was Semion Mikhailovich (as written in his Soviet passport, although his father had a different Jewish name). He was born in 1898. His parents, Abram-Mihel and Klara Avidon, were also from Ukraine, from the city of Dnepropetrovsk. It was a big, religious family, and they had six children—three boys and three girls. My father was the oldest in the family. Before the Revolution, my grandfather Abram-Mihel owned leather workshops or perhaps even a factory. He was a very tough person. He believed that girls did not need an education, and that it was useless for boys, too. In his opinion, the boys were better off helping their father, and that is what they did. Only the youngest one, attending the "workers" (evening) school, was able to obtain an education and become an engineer.

My parents were married in Moscow in 1929. For a year, they lived in Tashkent, doing chores for grandfather. Then my grandfather sent them, along with my father's brother and his family, to Leningrad for some family business where they remained. By that time, I had already been born.

I was born in Moscow in 1930. I was only four months old when I was brought to Leningrad, which is where I spent most of my adult life before leaving for Israel (except for being evacuated during World War II). We lived in a large communal apartment (*kommunalka*) [a communal apartment in which several families shared the same bathroom and kitchen facilities; it was formed by dividing up large pre-revolutionary apartments that the regime confiscated]; there were eight rooms, each housing a separate family. As there were many Jews among our neighbors, I did not feel the domestic antisemitism that flourished at that time in Leningrad. A big, religious Jewish family, the Hrapkovskys, originally from Belarus, also lived in that apartment. They came from the town of Nevel. There were six children, the youngest of whom was a boy, Boris, who was five years older than I was. It was they who helped

# Avidon Family Tree
## Ida Taratuta's branch

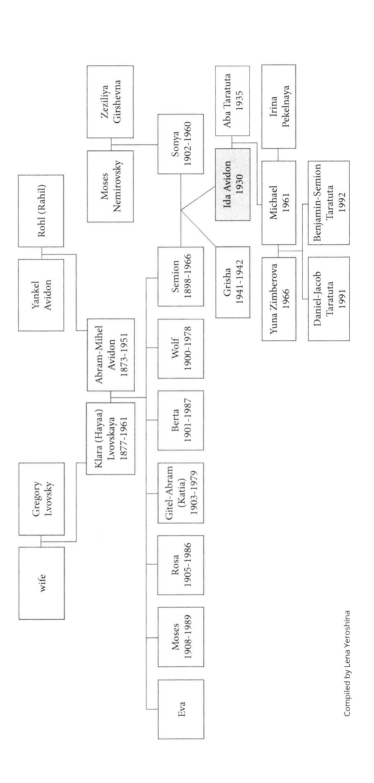

raise me. They explained to me how to behave in school and how to react to antisemitic insults. Therefore, from my early childhood, I knew who I was and what to do when I attended school.

My mother and father were not religious but, because of this family from Belarus, I saw how to lay tefillin (phylacteries) and what to do with a tallit. It was 1936–1938. I remember that the older sons were already members of the *Komsomol* (The Young Communists' League), but, when time came for Saturday prayers, the door was locked. I was permitted to be present. I actually spent a great deal of time with them because it was boring to be alone at home. I think that this Jewish family had a great influence on my life. When Boris (we called him Borya) was prepared for his bar mitzvah, the rabbi had to come to teach him Hebrew. Boris, however, said that without me he would not study. I would, therefore, come to lessons, sit near him quietly, and listen. (I was then 5–6 years old.) When the old rabbi, exhausted, fell asleep at the table, we would play outside.

I often participated in their family meals. Not necessarily because I was hungry, I just preferred their food. At home, I did not eat kasha (porridge) at all, but if at their house, I was asked: "Who wants kasha?" I would answer, "Yes, but without milk and butter." Sometimes my mother secretly brought the neighbors "our" kasha, but I always recognized it because it was made with a lot of milk and butter. In that family, everything was simple: the sour cabbage, porridge, potatoes and herring. Except for Saturdays, there was no tablecloth; instead, the weekday table was covered with newspaper. The newspaper was in Yiddish, and Boris said to me: "Come on, show me the letter 'aleph'" (the first letter of the Jewish alphabet). I found it, and it was my first lesson in Hebrew.

There were three sons and three daughters in the family. One of them was Debora, Doba as we called her. One member of her son's family later came to Israel, and found us. Doba, unfortunately, has long since died, but we still maintain friendly relations with her son's family. Recently, we were invited to his son's wedding.

## *Evacuation*

When Hitler attacked the USSR, I had finished the third grade. Early that morning, a distant cousin of my mother's, a cadet from the nearby Naval School, came over. He was very anxious and told us that he had come to say goodbye. Apparently, something had happened and the cadets were to be sent away somewhere. That very day, at twelve o'clock, we heard the speech by Foreign Minister Molotov, broadcast on the radio, announcing that on June 22, 1941, at four o'clock in the morning, German troops had treacherously attacked the Soviet Union without even a declaration of war.

Sometime after the war started, the order came to evacuate children of the age of kindergarten and primary school from Leningrad. I was supposed to be evacuated with my school, and my belongings were already at the school. At that time, we had a three-month-old brother in my family, and my mother was instructed to travel with the infant. My parents, however, decided it would be better if I went with my mother and brother. Early in the morning, we went to school, where I was crossed off the list and retrieved my things.

My mother and I went to the Yaroslav region by special train, and my father remained in Leningrad. We settled in the village of Great Pogulyanka, where the locals did not greet us very warmly. I was not bored there because, in the same village, I discovered many of the children from our large building in Leningrad. It was the end of July, and in August, my father was taken into the army. Shortly before, my grandfather, my mother's father, moved from Moscow to Leningrad after the death of my grandmother. When father went to the front, my grandfather joined us in the village.

Toward the end of that summer, my father was sent to Yaroslavl for some military courses, and on the way there, he was able to visit us. Father tried to persuade my mother to move to the Gorky region, to which his parents and sisters had been evacuated. "What are you doing alone?" he asked. "In difficult times you all have to be together." The next day, my father put us all on a small ship, and we sailed in the direction of the town of Pavlovo. There we settled in the village Tumbotino, where we met my father's numerous relatives. But we did not stay long. I did not even go to school there. As the Germans approached Moscow, it was necessary to seek some other haven, to escape the rapidly advancing German army.

We remembered that some distant relatives lived in the Urals, in the town of Nizhny Tagil, so we decided that we should all go there. On November 16, 1941, we arrived at the wharf in Pavlovo, where we were supposed to board a ship to Kazan. I remember the date well, because that same day the Germans almost reached Moscow, which created terrible panic. Many Muscovites were leaving the city on foot, and among them was the husband of my father's sister. He went along with the employees of his factory (the machinery was transported in vehicles). In the forest, they unexpectedly met my father, whose military unit had come under bombardment. Many died, others were scattered throughout the forest. They tried to persuade my father to go along with the factory group, but he refused, as he did not want to become a deserter. They went on, and at the quay at Pavlovo, they suddenly saw us and gave us greetings from my father. It was just like in the movies!

I still remember the harrowing scenes that we saw as we sat for three long days at the quay waiting to board the steamer. There was a continuous stream of cars and buses with the wives and children of party leaders and other bosses. Well-groomed women in furs, with huge suitcases, walked across the shaky planks to the steamer. Some even tried to bring furniture. I remember a piano being dropped into the water; nobody even tried to get it out. There was terrible panic and fear that the Germans would bomb us. And we, along with other refugees, were sitting and waiting.

Finally, on the third day, they put us on a huge barge that was then towed into the middle of the river and just left there. It was terribly cold; the water in the river began to freeze, and people feared that the barge would not be able to move. Moreover, the barge was in fact unfit to carry passengers. These were appalling conditions: it was impossible even to swaddle the child. My little brother caught a cold.

For an entire day, our barge stood in the middle of the river when, finally, we were taken in tow and started to move. I do not remember how long we traveled, first by river and then by rail. Eventually, we brought the sick infant to Nizhny Tagil. Unfortunately, he was fading and nothing could be done. I remember the night when my brother stopped breathing; my mother began to scream: "Grisha geshtorben!" ("Grisha is dead" in Yiddish). Clearly, in extreme situations, a person turns to their native language. There was no effective treatment for pneumonia in those days, and ever since then, I have always feared this disease.

In Nizhny Tagil, we lived under very difficult conditions; there was real hunger. To survive somehow, my mother sold the things that we had been able to bring with us. We rented a room where my mother, my grandfather, and I lived, along with our landlady. The worst thing for me was that this landlady had a disabled child, a fourteen-year-old boy who was developmentally only four years of age. I was afraid to come home after school.

We lived there for about six months. Then mother made contact with her cousin, who had evacuated to Kazakhstan, and we decided to go to her in Central Asia, to the city of Jambul. We had money because my mother had worked in Nizhny Tagil, but it was impossible to buy tickets. My mother therefore bought some bottles of vodka and gave them to the conductors, and they let us into the railroad car. It was already 1942.

In Jambul, mother immediately obtained a job as a typist working for the municipality. Her salary enabled us to buy flour, bread, and rice, in addition to the meager rations that our ration cards provided. There were ration cards for bread and other food products (just as there were in the United States during World War II), but those items were not always available. A ration card looked like a book of postage stamp–sized coupons. To buy a product, you needed first to cut one off from your card in exchange for the right to purchase (you could not buy anything without a coupon). Fortunately, fruits and vegetables in that southern land were in abundance, and most important, it was warm there.

We lived in Jambul until 1944. I thought at the time that it was an eternity.

### Return to Leningrad

In 1944, my mother learned that a Leningrad representative was recruiting new workers for a jute factory. The siege that the city had suffered was already over, but so many people had died of starvation that there were not enough workers. This was our only way to return home; in Leningrad there was not enough to eat and refugees were allowed back only for essential businesses. My mother therefore signed up for the jute factory

We traveled there in a freight car; the trip took more than a month. The train was not following any timetable; it moved only when the way was clear.

Mother was initially sent to work as a cleaner. The conditions were horrendous. The factory produced hemp bags and she would come home from work all white with hemp dust; it was impossible to take a bath because we had to heat water on a kerosene stove. Then someone discovered that mother could type, and they soon moved her to the factory administration, where she worked until 1945, when my father returned from the army.

When we were still in evacuation, a woman whose building had been bombed moved into our communal room. Our neighbors, with whom we were on good terms despite the close quarters, wrote to us about it. When the Leningrad siege was over, mother wrote to our neighbors asking them to open up our room, sell some of our belongings and send us the proceeds as we were short of money. My father was a simple soldier and allowances were paid only to the families of officers. If soldiers were injured, they were treated in hospitals for free.

After returning to Leningrad, my mother did not want to own "things," even necessary things. The war had changed her values. She explained that belongings were nothing in comparison to human life. When I married Aba, his grandmother said to me, "Why didn't your parents see to it that you had your own living space?" Yes, it was so. Having experienced the horrors of war and evacuation, my parents did not care about material wealth.

During our evacuation, I had graduated from sixth grade, but we returned in November, and it was too late for the beginning of the school year. My mother worked from dawn to dusk, and I myself went to register for school. The principal persuaded me to go through the program of the sixth grade again because she was not sure of the education that I received in Jambul.

I began to study in a school for girls on Chaikovsky Street. (Girls and boys studied separately, from the years of World War II until 1954). It was the former palace of Prince Oldenburg. There was a wonderful library of birch wood, an assembly hall with a white marble fireplace, a portrait of the Empress, and a beautiful hardwood floor. Everything was gorgeous, except for the classrooms, which were located somewhere in the attic, in the former servants' rooms. In our class, there were many Jewish girls, and thus there was no antisemitism, but most of us were anti-Soviet. I remember once, when I was visiting a new school friend, her mother came out of the bath, which they had installed in the kitchen, and said, "For the first time during Soviet rule, I have actually enjoyed something."

I remember Victory Day, May 9, and the universal rejoicing. It seemed that now everything would be fine. But my grandfather died on May 17; he had so wanted to enjoy the victory....

## *The University*

In 1949, I graduated from high school and enrolled in the English Department of the Pedagogical Institute. I originally tried, unsuccessfully, to enter the Foreign Language Institute, also in the English Department. Aba and I experienced many similar situations in our life. In his own entrance exam in Russian Literature, he failed the written paper, and I almost failed the written exam for the same reason. During the oral examination in literature, I was shown my written work. I was horrified to see that it was all marked in red ink. When I was able to scrutinize it, I realized that there was, in effect, only one mistake: I occasionally forgot to put a period at the end of a sentence. The examiner inserted the missing periods and even circled them to make them more noticeable.

In short, I was not awarded a passing mark. When I came out into the hallway after the announcement of the exam results, all the Jewish girls were there. We looked at each other and laughed. It was all too obvious. Someone said: "Well, okay, let them choke on their university! Let us go to the Pedagogical Institute!" And we all went there.

At the Pedagogical Institute, the entrance examinations continued, and we were promised that we would be accepted based upon our grades. Nevertheless, I had to find friends, or acquaintances of friends, to help with enrollment; there were too many candidates. I was helped by the assistant dean of the university, who had helped many of us. He did this not for money or gifts, but simply from a feeling of Jewish solidarity.

Our group consisted of ten people, four of us Jewish. I made friends with Mila Gedroits, who had also failed in her examinations at the Foreign Language Institute; she was the daughter of a "repressed" person. Her father, a Pole, was a prominent engineer. He was arrested and executed in 1937, and her mother was deported to Central Asia. After high school, Mila was sent by her mother to study in Leningrad and live with her grandmother. This grandmother just happened to be a neighbor of Aba's cousin, Alexander (Sasha).

I thus met my future husband in a communal apartment.

When Aba started to work at the classified research organization where I worked as a translator of scientific and technical literature, we became friends. There we mixed with a very good, mostly Jewish, group of youth. The military authorities had apparently been given no instructions about the "Fifth paragraph"[1], and the political officer treated Jews decently in general.

## In Bashkirostan

After graduating university, I was sent to work in Bashkirostan, to a small industrial town, called Chernikhovsk, near Ufa. I worked there as an English language teacher in a boys' school. This was in 1953. Many Jews, exiled there under Stalin, were living in Chernikhovsk. In our school, there were even some teachers who had been posted there as early as the 1920s and 1930s.

I had to work there for two years, after which I was allowed to return to Leningrad.

## Marriage and birth of our son

In 1960, I married Aba. The joy of marriage was overtaken, however, by the sudden death of my mother after an unsuccessful operation for a strangulated hernia. She was only 57 years old. My father did not outlive her for long; he died in 1966 of a stroke. In 1961, our son Michael (Misha) was born.

## Application for repatriation

In June 1967, the Six-Day War in Israel aroused the Jews in the USSR. From mere opponents to the Soviet regime, we turned into real Zionists. After the

---

[1]   The fifth point in the passport specified a nationality, in this case *evrei* (Jew); Jews were often subject to discrimination because of their nationality.—*Editor's note*.

Leningrad Airplane Hijackers Trial,[2] we started to think about repatriation. (Based on the UN Universal Declaration of Human Rights, to which the Soviet Union was a signatory, we, as Jews, had the "right" to return to our homeland, which helped lay the legal foundation for our right to immigrate or repatriate to our homeland, Israel.)

It was 1970–1971. To apply for exit visas while working in so-called "secret" organizations was pointless. We first had to "dry out," that is, leave our jobs, and then start a countdown when we no longer were engaged in classified "secret" work. In other words, we would have to wait a year or two.

Meanwhile, *aliya* (immigration) to Israel was increasing. Our friends Svetlana and Alex Belinsky asked for an invitation from Israel and began to prepare for departure. This greatly influenced us. We therefore decided not to wait and we announced our intentions, although we understood that they would not let us leave immediately. It was 1971, but we decided to apply for an exit visa anyway. At that time, it meant that we had a lot to lose, such as jobs, friends, and social life.

In the summer of 1972, we both left our "secret" organizations. Because of antisemitism, I could not find a professional job as a translator or teacher. Expressing one's desire to leave our "beautiful country" put one into the category of "traitor," and thereby not entitled to teach Soviet children. I therefore found a job in the post office as a mail sorter, and Aba took a course to become a taxi driver.

We did not yet have the necessary invitation from Israel, and to request it could create problems. It could be done through those who had already left the country, but often their notebooks or address books were confiscated at Customs. It was also possible to ask foreign tourists to provide an invitation, but in the early 1970s, there were not so many of them in Leningrad. To call Israel by telephone was just impossible; from Leningrad, there were only two calls a day. It was also a problem to request the invitation by mail because letters did not always reach Israel, and not everyone had the courage to choose this option.

---

[2]  The case of an attempt to seize a small passenger plane by a group of Zionists from Riga and Leningrad who planned to escape from the USSR to reach Israel. The trial of the "Airplane Hijackers" took place in December 1970.—*Editor's note.*

At that time, our friends, the Belinskys, received permission to leave the country. On the eve of their departure, I took a piece of white cloth and wrote on it in ink our passport data, together with that of our friends and other Jews who wanted to leave. I sewed this scrap under the lining of Sasha's jacket. Soft fabric cannot be detected during a casual personal search. Thus, he managed to smuggle his jacket with all its information through customs, not only with our data, but also with a whole list of people who wanted to receive an invitation from Israel.

The invitation reached us in the beginning of 1973. In order to apply for repatriation, however, we needed references from work. For this purpose, I had to undergo a general meeting, which had the purpose of enabling fellow workers to severely condemn me as a "traitor." This was a typical Soviet method of discouraging people from leaving.

Aba, without having to endure this charade of a meeting, obtained a "character reference" from the management of our residence because he was briefly unemployed at the time. Fortunately, at my classified work, we had a decent director, so my "condemnation" was relatively mild.

In August 1973, we received our first refusal, which was not unexpected. When the chief of OVIR (Department of Visas and Registrations), Bokov, saw our papers, he said, "What are you thinking? Both of you were working in secret (classified) organizations; who would let you emigrate?" At the exit of the OVIR offices, Jewish activists recorded the names of new "refuseniks." They already had a list of twenty-six families; we became the twenty-seventh.

Becoming refuseniks meant a new lifestyle: We started to sign collective letters of protest, meet with other Jews who were in the same "suspended" state, and share information (about our lives, about underground lectures, about how to receive invitations from Israel, how to apply for exit visas, and so on). There was certain solidarity among us. We did not yet know what awaited us during the nearly fifteen years of living in refusal; that our son Misha would be drafted into the Soviet army, and the many other difficulties we were to encounter. Over these years, however, we gained many wonderful and devoted friends on both sides of the ocean, and most of them are still with us.

I will give you two typical examples from that time.

Our friend Yakov Rabinovich, who lived alone in a large two-bedroom apartment, nobly offered to switch with us for our cramped one-bedroom apartment. It was a generous offer, which we, of course, could not accept.

The family of Alya and Sergey Yuzvinsky proposed an even more risky step. Receiving permission to leave in 1979, they offered to marry their daughter Katie to our son in a fictitious marriage to get him out of the country. It was obvious to us that not only would Misha not receive permission to leave, but also Katie, in marrying him, would lose her opportunity to emigrate. And who knows when her parents would see their daughter again? We, of course, could not accept such a sacrifice, and the Yuzvinsky family safely emigrated.

# 2.

# Grandfather Aba

## The history of the Taratuta family

A fragment, as told by Mordechai Benyamini[3] (Taratuta) and written (in Hebrew) by his niece Tova Arieli, on the forty-first anniversary of the death of her grandfather Benyamin.

The family originated in the town of Chudnov in Ukraine. The paterfamilias was Mordechai (born 1820), whose parents died in his youth, leaving him an orphan. He was then sent to a stepbrother who was a *dayan* (a religious judge) in the town of Bershad. The stepbrother was asked to care for the child, but he ignored his responsibilities to the orphan. A relative who lived in the Ukrainian village Sobodovna took the child into his home and raised him. This relative worked on a rented farm.

He was wealthy and the father of both sons and daughters. There was a Lithuanian religious student living in his home who served as a teacher to this man's children. The children's interests did not, however, center round studies, as they were more interested in the farm, the horses, and playing games. When Mordechai was brought to the house, and the Lithuanian student noticed the boy's intellectual prowess, he invested his time in him. He progressed rapidly along the lines of the Lithuanian style of study.

Over the years, this wealthy man married off one of his sons and invited his relative, the dayan from Bershad and the orphan's stepbrother, to attend the wedding. The learned student and the dayan argued the finer points of the Torah and *halakha* (religious law). The Lithuanian student–teacher pressured the dayan in his questioning

---

[3] Mordechai Benyamini passed away in the beginning of 1990. His father Binyamin (uncle of Tova Arieli) was born in 1852 and lived a long life.

and the latter had difficulty in answering. The orphan Mordechai, who had already reached the age of sixteen, was thus called upon to participate in the religious argument. Mordechai's responses were exceptionally well informed, at which point, the dayan was told that Mordechai was in fact his stepbrother. The Lithuanian student accused the dayan of having neglected his duty to his stepbrother. The connection between them remained cold and distant, however.

The relative who had adopted him treated Mordechai as if he were his own son. When the time came for him to be conscripted into the tsar's army, his release was purchased by buying the name of a person who had died but whose name had not been registered as having passed away: this was the norm in those days. (People deliberately did not notify the authorities of somebody's death in order to make use of the dead person's name). In this way, Mordechai received the last name of Taratuta; his original name was forgotten over time and, until today, remains a mystery.

His adoptive family married Mordechai to a respectable woman who could work while Mordechai concentrated on his Torah studies. The wife's name was Dovrash (Tova), from the town of Kananela, in the Cherkassy Region and it was there that they established themselves. Mordechai studied and Tova ran a shop, providing the family with an income.

Mordechai did not live long and left Tova with five children: Tama, the eldest daughter, Binyamin, Yeshika/Yehoshua, Shmuel-Aba, and Krisel, the youngest. Dovrash (Tova) was unable to provide them with an education because of the necessity of earning a living for the family. They were all good people, honest and just, but there were no more Talmudic scholars. All the children established their own families.

The third son of Mordechai and Dovrash was named Yeshika/Yehoshua. He married Cherna, and they had eleven children, of whom I remember only the names Eli, Motel, Yitshak, Moshe, Rizel, and Dovrash. The youngest son, Shmuel Aba, married Golda, and they had five sons. One of them, Moshe, was killed by bandits. Another, Gdalia, also met a violent death. The rest fought with the Red Army and stayed in Russia. In 1988, Shmuel Aba's grandson, also called Aba, came to Israel.

The fourth daughter, Krisel, married David Portnyak, and they had two children, Motel, who was killed during the pogroms in Russia, and Batya, who married Moshe Lores. They went to America and had two daughters, Marilyn and Thelma.

## My father Yakov (Yankel)

One of the children of the family's founder, Shmuel Aba Taratuta, was my grandfather on my father's side. My father himself was born in 1897 in Uman. This was a well-known *shtetl* (small town) in the Kiev province, where the famous Hassidic *tsadik* (righteous man), Rabbi Nachman of Bratslav, was buried. Now every year on Rosh Hashanah thousands of Hasidim from all over the world (and, of course, from Israel) come to this place to pray at his tomb.

My father's name was Ya'akov Abramovich (as it was written in his Soviet passport), but his real Jewish name was Yankel-Moshe-Shmuel-Aba. Father was from an educated family but he himself had no higher education. He worked, I think, as a supplier at some factory, and later, after World War II, at a department store. He had three brothers, one in Leningrad, one in Moscow, one in Odessa, and a sister, Tanya, who died of starvation during the siege of Leningrad. In the early 1930s, my father left Uman for Leningrad, and he soon married my mother; he was already thirty-seven years old at the time.

## My mother Fanya

My parents were not religious. Mother was much younger than father; she was born in 1910 in Kiev. Her maiden name was Fanya Grigoryevna Epstein. Kiev was outside of the Pale of Settlement for Jews, but some categories of Jews were allowed to live there. For example, college graduates, teachers, doctors, as well as the merchants of the First Guild. My maternal great-grandfather was a teacher in a *yeshiva* and therefore he and his family were allowed to live in Kiev. Mother worked at various jobs such as a print shop typist and a pharmacy cashier.

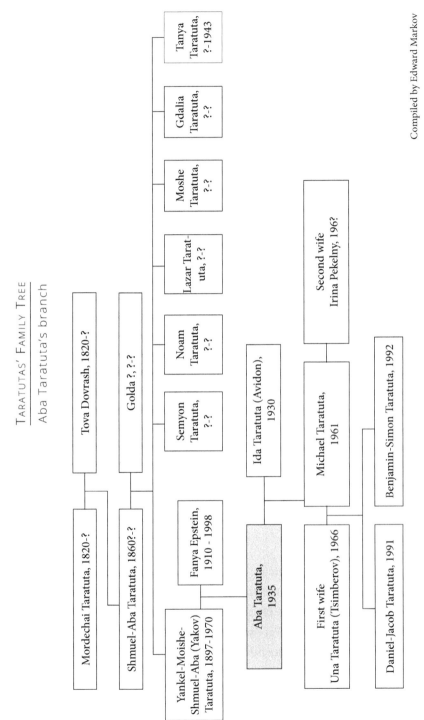

Compiled by Edward Markov

## *My grandmother Adele*

My maternal grandmother was Adele Avrutskaya (Epstein) who was born in Kiev in 1879. Her Yiddish was better than her Russian, and she always preferred speaking Yiddish with those who understood it. She often talked with my mother in Yiddish, especially if I was around and they did not want me to know what they were talking about. I guess, that's why my command of Yiddish is not too bad even now.

Grandma Adele had three children: Emil (his birth name was Shmuel Yosef Gershkowitz), Isaac (Yosef-Isaac), and my mother Fanya. She brought them up all by herself, because she and her husband were divorced.

My favorite uncle, Emil, had to start working from an early age to help his brother Isaac pay for his education; he also supported Grandma Adele financially all her life, right up to her death. He himself had no time to start a family and remained a bachelor for many years.

Every year, my grandmother organized Passover Seders at her home, and I remember Uncle Emil saying "Ma nishtana," It seems to me that this was the only Hebrew he knew. Grandma told us that her father knew Shalom Aleichem, and that the famous Jewish writer had even attended many parties at their home in Kiev. She used to say, "All the horrible things happening around us happen only because Comrade Stalin does not know about them. Let me go to him and I'll tell him what is going on and how we live." What amazing ideas my grandmother had about the leader and teacher of the Soviet people, the "best friend of Soviet sportsmen and all of progressive humankind."

## *Grandmother's brothers*

At the beginning of the Great Patriotic War (World War II), one of my grandmother's brothers, Moisey (Moishe), was enlisted and sent to the front, but in the first days of the war, he was wounded in the knee and hospitalized. Afterwards, his leg would not bend for the rest of his life. Naturally, he was no longer fit for military service.

The name of my grandmother's other brother was Yosif. He had a son, Yakov, who was also at the front. The Germans captured Yakov, but, having a very dark complexion, he pretended to be a Karaite (the Caucasian nationality), which saved his life. Because he knew German, the Germans used him as an interpreter. He then fled to the partisans and fought in a guerrilla detachment. The head of his unit was an antisemite who took a dislike to him. When the Soviet troops arrived, the commander informed on Yakov, saying that he was a collaborator. Yakov was arrested and sentenced to ten years in a forced labor camp in the Gulag. He was lucky that the judge was a Jew and did not give him the death penalty, as was customary in those days. This happened at the end of the war. As far as I know, the Gulag camp where Yakov spent his time was located somewhere in Vorkuta. After his release, he lost the right to live in large cities. Yakov remained in that area for some time and got married. When he was allowed to return to Leningrad, he already had three children.

## Other relatives

I have a cousin, Alexander Epstein, the oldest son of my Uncle Isaac. Alexander (Sasha) and his wife Luba still live in Leningrad but visit Israel every year because their son Yury has been living here since the early 1990s. Uncle Isaac's other son, Alexander's brother Anatoly, has been living in Israel with his wife Clara since 1977. There are more cousins. One, Alec Taratuta, from Odessa, now lives in the U.S. In Russia, he was afraid to have any contact with us, especially after some articles about me appeared in the newspapers.

In Moscow, I have cousins from my father's side: Ella Alexandrovsky (Taratuta), who was born in 1930, and her sister Svetlana Smirnova (Taratuta), who was born in 1938. Both have visited us here in Israel. Ida's cousin Erik Avidon lives in Leningrad, and his son Roman, in Israel.

Incidentally, many of my distant relatives have been living in Israel for many years, some since 1919. One of them, Tova Arieli, wrote the book on the genealogy of our family and compiled our family tree. I have that book in Hebrew.

## American relatives (from my mother's side)

My grandmother's sister, Haya-Itta, and her husband, Gary (Grisha) Weil, emigrated from Russia in 1914, even before World War I. Haya-Itta was only twenty-one at that time. She left, but Grandma Adele remained in Russia: she was much older and by this time already had three children. Grandma said that leaving the country was very easy: you simply pay the district police official five rubles for an international passport and go wherever you want.

In the U.S., Haya-Itta gave birth to two daughters: Rose Robbins and Francesca. Rose Robbins had a daughter, Dana. Before World War II, Grandma Adele corresponded with them, and in 1936, Haya-Itta visited Leningrad to see her sister.

My second cousin Dana, when she was a law student, was an intern in a firm of lawyers, one of whose clients was Irene Manikovsky, one of the first leaders of the Union of Council for Soviet Jews. In 1974, Irene visited us in Leningrad. Dana had found our name by chance in the list of refuseniks and connected us with her family. They visited with us in Israel, and we have remained in contact ever since.

## Evacuation

I was born in 1935 in Leningrad, and, except for three years of evacuation, I continued to live there. As we were on vacation in the town of Korostyshev in Ukraine when Hitler invaded the Soviet Union on June 22, 1941, it was very difficult for us to return to Leningrad. My father was not at the front. He came to the recruitment office and began to cough in the face of the military commissar, saying that he had tuberculosis. This got him released from military service. Uncle Emil had a "white ticket" (an exemption from military service) because of a duodenal ulcer, and Uncle Isaac used his brother Emil's documents in order also to receive an exemption. Our family thus did not prove to be very patriotic.

In August 1941, my entire family went to the city of Troitsk in the Southern Urals. It did not matter to us where we went, but an elderly distant relative of my aunt Pauline, the wife of Uncle Isaac, lived in Troitsk. When boarding the train, one had to take the train cars by storm, our luggage was thrown through the window, and then we fought to get through the doors. This happened on August 24, 1941, but the train did not depart until the following morning. As we found out later, German bombers hit the train that had departed earlier. We also saw Germans planes circling above us, but this time no bombs were dropped. It took us about three weeks to reach the town of Troitsk.

By Russian standards, it was a small city with single-story wooden houses. The only two-story stone building was occupied by the district police department. We rented a room in a three-room house. Our landlady lived in one of the rooms, she rented another room to a Tatar family with three children, and we occupied the third room. There were five of us living in that room: my parents, Uncle Emil, Grandmother Adele, and myself.

In the backyard, there were winter sheds for the cattle. In the summer, cows from different households were herded into one flock to graze together. First, we bought a goat, but then we traded this goat, plus two "cuts" (a few yards of fabric) we had brought with us, for a cow. My mother took care of the cow. It gave only a couple of liters of milk a day and was exchanged for another one, which gave even less. Finally, we got a third cow, which gave about 12 liters. From this milk, we made sour cream and butter, and as a result, there was no milk left for sale. Later the cow gave birth to a calf. For two weeks, we kept the calf in the same room in which we lived, and then it was traded in for milk.

My father found work at a factory. Uncle Emil, who lived with us, worked at a felt boots factory. He was the only one in the whole family who was eligible for the white (wheat) bread ration because of his duodenal ulcer. He eventually underwent surgery at the local hospital, which was very successful. Before the war, a famous Moscow surgeon Professor Riss had promised to operate on his ulcer on condition that "there would be no war" (as he put it).

Uncle Isaac and his family lived separately from us. By training, he was a civil engineer, and he found a job in his profession. During the war, those of us who were evacuated found various methods of making extra money. I did likewise. There was food rationing by a system of ration cards. There were cards for bread and other food products, which were by no means always available. A ration card looked like a book of postage stamp–sized coupons. To buy a product, you first had to cut off a coupon from your card in exchange for the right to buy; nothing could be bought without the coupon. The store had to return these coupons to the government accounting office, and for convenience, they were glued onto sheets of paper; this was my job.

The first time I encountered antisemitism occurred immediately after our arrival in Troitsk. I was six years old, walking down the street, and I ran into a group of girls and boys. One girl, much older than I was, was probably their leader. They beat me lightly, explaining why and for what reason. It was my first lesson in Zionism, and I am very grateful to them for this. I received the second lesson in the first grade at school, which I entered in 1943 at the age of eight (in Leningrad, pupils constantly insulted me, teased and mocked me as a *zhid* [a disrespectful word for "Jew"]).

Even in the boondocks of Troitsk, there was at least one Jewish house of worship. Every Yom Kippur, my grandmother Adele, who fasted on that day, went there to pray. There was another interesting phenomenon—a fraternity of Polish Jews. During the war, many Polish Jews fled from the German occupation to the Soviet Union. Some of them, most of them members of the Zionist movement, Beitar, were, of course, dispatched into exile or forced into labor camps, but others were allowed to remain. Polish Jews received material support, perhaps through the Joint organization. The chairman of the group distributed this aid. We became friends with several families. They tried to maintain the same lifestyle as they had had in Poland, and somehow they succeeded. I do not know how. One of them, Krakowiak by name, once invited us to dinner, which consisted of several dishes and was served by a housekeeper. This made a lasting impression on me. At the first opportunity, all of them left, some even during the war.

My Uncle Emil was a remarkable man, a righteous person, although he was not religious. He fell in love with a lovely Polish girl, who was in Troitsk with her father. She agreed to marry him, but stipulated one condition; my uncle would have to leave for Poland with her. However, my grandmother did not give him permission, and our grandmother was the "absolute dictator" of the family. She gave orders not only to her children and grandchildren, but also to her brothers, sisters, and cousins. As a result, Uncle Emil remained a bachelor almost until the end of his days.

## Return to Leningrad

We spent about three years (1941–1944) in Troitsk and then returned to Leningrad, which was not such a simple undertaking. Part of the Soviet regime was a system of registration—*propiska*. This meant that no one was free to choose his own place of residence; everyone had to obtain permission from the local authorities. Even though our family had lived in Leningrad before the war, in order to be eligible to return, our men had to be recruited to work in a small town near Leningrad.

We traveled in a cargo car that had been used in peacetime for the transport of goods or cattle. About ten families were put into an empty boxcar; their belongings were piled up there, and they slept on them. The train moved slowly, stopping and standing for a long time at the stations. The journey lasted three weeks.

Upon our arrival in Leningrad, we first settled in the room of my grandmother's brother Moisey. Two of the rooms in this communal apartment, which housed nine families, were occupied by a family that had stayed in Leningrad throughout the siege. As far as I know, this family was fairly decent, and at first, they allowed us to stay in one room, later releasing the second one for us. We lived in those rooms for thirteen years, until 1957.

In Leningrad, I felt the full force of antisemitism not only on the streets, but also in my school. We lived on Ligovskaya Street in a district that had been famous for its crime since tsarist times. Hooligans were plentiful in my grade and throughout the school. They constantly insulted, bullied, and beat me. At the time, I was short on fighting skills. As I was the only Jew in my class, it was impossible to cope; it was simply dangerous to go to school. My parents decided to transfer me to another school, one located in a very prestigious area downtown, although by the end of the war, the homeless were living down the manholes in that same area. I studied there from the second grade to the tenth grade. In this school, the situation was quite normal and there were many Jewish children in my class. In fact, at graduation, half of my classmates were either Jewish or half Jewish. Mine was an all-boys school. I graduated in 1953, but coeducation, as far as I remember, started only in 1954, a year later.

My grades were not bad. I did not have excellent marks in all subjects, but I was good at math, and I even participated in the Math Olympics. Those who had the highest marks in most of the subjects usually received a gold or silver medal. In 1953, Stalin died, but, as his ethos was still alive, no medals were given out in our class, in spite of the fact that there was one boy, Averbookh, who had the highest marks in all the subjects. Incidentally, he was half Jewish and an antisemite at the same time. Sometimes this happens.

School education in Russia was not too bad, but this was true only in big cities. In rural areas, the graduates usually had very little training, even those with gold medals.

## *The University*

I applied to the Department of Astronomy of the Mathematics and Mechanics Faculty at Leningrad University. To be accepted, you had to pass eight exams on different subjects: one inadequate mark and you were out. That is what I received on the first written exam, for my essay on literature. Of course, it was a blow because there was a danger of being called up to the army (in the USSR, there was compulsory military service), and I did not want to serve. University students were exempt from military service because there were military departments in almost all universities so that students could study military science and receive an officer's rank after graduation. After this, from time to time, they served for a month or two as reservists, but this is not the same as serving two to three years as a private.

I spent two days in shock, and then I appealed to the university's commission. When I arrived at the commission, there were nine additional people and all of them were Jews. I was invited to an interview, and the teacher who checked my work showed me my essay, all covered with red pencil marks. *Wow,* I thought, *how many errors!* It turned out that a period at the end of one of my sentences was not clear enough; this was an error! Errors in the crossed-out text were also counted as mistakes. I was saved by one woman in the commission who said that my essay deserved a satisfactory mark. This enabled me to take other exams, but I had already lost considerable time, and I had only fourteen days to pass the remaining seven exams.

The next exam was in physics. It was the subject I knew best because I had had a very experienced tutor, a university professor. When I was preparing to answer the questions in my exam, a fellow who was sitting beside me asked me to help him. I solved a very easy problem for him and found out later that he received an excellent mark.

There were three examiners in the room. I chose the one who looked the least disapproving. He took a look at my exam paper, asked about my strange name, and why my exam sheet was different. When I explained to him about the family name, two other examiners immediately flocked to us. I quickly answered the questions on my ticket, after which the three of them asked me very tricky questions for an hour, maybe more. They were very surprised when I gave correct answers to all of them!

I do not know; perhaps they did not have specific questions prepared for such a case, or maybe they did not expect that I would answer all the questions. In any case, they could do nothing but give me a satisfactory mark. Incidentally, there were subjects for which I was not prepared very well—chemistry, for example. It was apparent, however, that they had been told to give me a failing mark in this particular subject.

In the written exam in mathematics, among all the matriculating students, I was the only one who solved all the problems. Even this, however, did not save me; my average score ended up being slightly lower than the entrance score. My Uncle Isaac, who knew the Vice Rector of the University, thus negotiated with him to permit me to attend classes as a "student candidate" in the group of astronomers, and if I were to pass all the exams after the first semester with good grades, I would be accepted. I did this, thus becoming a full-time student at Leningrad University.

There were some very talented men who were taking exams in my group among the matriculates; one of them even knew mathematics at a level far beyond the school course. He was failed, however, precisely in mathematics. I know that in Moscow University at that time, there was a special team of examiners whose main task was to not allow Jewish youngsters to pass the entrance exams to the Faculty of Mechanics and Mathematics.

In 1958, I graduated from the university with a degree in radio astronomy.

I did my work for graduation in the Pulkovo Observatory near Leningrad and expected to work there after graduation. In the Soviet Union at that time, there was a system of "distribution," that is, assigning young professionals to work in their specialty for at least three years. (They were not allowed to leave the assigned jobs before the three years had expired.) When I came to the distribution commission, however, nothing was offered to me at first. I was then asked to leave the room, so they could consult. When I returned, I was offered a job at the Izhora Plant. It was a heavy-industry plant, and it had nothing to do with astronomy. I asked, "What do you mean, 'Izhora plant'? This is not my specialty." There was a noise in the room: "You not satisfied? It's only 40 minutes by train from Leningrad! We could also send you to the Far East!"

I had not agreed to sign the distribution paper, but I was told that it did not matter whether I signed it or not.

In the autumn of 1957, the first Soviet space satellite was launched, and at the Mathematics and Mechanics Department, a special team of radio astronomers was created to monitor the satellite. The team leader, Professor Alexander Shiryaev, was a very honest but naive man. He did not quite understand the country he was living in or the attitude of that country to Jews. He knew that I had not been "distributed," and he offered me work on his team, which, of course, I accepted. He took my papers and went to the personnel department of the university. There he was told that the distribution had already been completed and to make a change would be very difficult. "Now, if Taratuta had had a release from distribution..." they said to him.

Of course, he did not understand what the real reason was.

I went to the Izhora Plant to receive a release from the assignment, approached the personnel department and asked:

"Could you please let me go, as I am really not needed here?"

"Not needed? On the contrary, we have the Heavy Industry Design Bureau here, and they desperately need engineers and mathematicians."

Well, if nothing could be done, what was I supposed to do? I was very upset and went for a vacation to the Crimea, returning to Leningrad only in the late summer.

## After the University

Now what was I to do? As I needed a job, I went back to the Izhora plant. However, when I arrived there, there was a completely different situation: the bureau chief was absent and his deputy did not know what to do with me. I, therefore, returned to the personnel department, and they sent me to the foundry. When I got to the foundry, an elderly foreman with a big moustache, who looked like Taras Bulba, one of Gogol's characters, met me. I explained the situation to him, and he told me: "First, you have to spend about nine months here as an apprentice, and then we'll see what to do with you."

I asked, "Maybe you don't really need me here?"

"No, not really," he said.

"OK, then maybe you can write here on my referral form that you don't need me and sign it?"

Without too much hesitation, he did what I asked.

I, thus, went back to the personnel department and got my "free diploma," which meant that I was now free to start the job hunting all by myself, but I did not go back to the University. I was too proud for that.

One of my relatives advised me to apply for a vacant position in a classified[4] research organization, where he himself worked. Ironically, I received an offer (which I accepted, of course) and was assigned to the second level of security.

This organization did not produce anything and only did consulting work. In the backyard, there was a marine hydrological buoy, which was either stolen from the Americans or simply abandoned by them, and its contents were long and carefully studied. A political officer, who was in charge of personnel, was interested more in their training and professional prospects, rather than in their nationality. This was very unusual for that time and place, and as a result, there were many Jews working there. All the bosses there were naval officers, some of them writing PhD dissertations in naval science. I worked for two years in this organization and learned how to play ping-pong, volleyball, and chess with a clock (in school I took a great interest in checkers, and even achieved first-class status). From time to time, I did, of course, do some engineering work; for example, I took part, when second-level security was required, in the testing of several gadgets.

In 1960, I married Ida, and in 1961, our son Misha was born. In 1960, I found a normal job in another classified organization as an engineer-mathematician and worked there until 1964, when I changed my job for the third time. In my third job, I worked as a group leader up to 1972, when Ida and I made a decision to leave for Israel. Before that, however, I started postgraduate studies by correspondence course.

## Returning to Judaism

When I was still a freshman at university I decided to learn Yiddish. At that time, I did not really know the difference between Yiddish and Hebrew; I did not know that such a language as Ivrit (Hebrew) even existed. I did not know

---

4    In some so-called closed organizations, permission was required to access classified documents and information. Not all secret organizations had official legal names. They were designated by postal address such as a mail box number.—*Editor's note.*

any Hebrew teachers, but my grandmother knew Yiddish, which was her first language. When I asked her to teach me Yiddish, she gave me my first lesson but I did not continue beyond that.

A brilliant victory for Israel in the Six-Day War, during which, incidentally, the Soviet Union had provided every possible assistance to the Arabs, led many Soviet Jews to think seriously about immigrating to their historic homeland. In addition, after the Soviet invasion of Czechoslovakia in 1968, we realized that the regime in the Soviet Union had become so harsh that there was no future for the Jews in this country. We came to this conclusion on our own: Ida and I had no spiritual leaders at that time, except for my grandmother, who still tried to keep up Jewish traditions in her house, and our Jewish friends from Riga.

Each summer, in the years from 1948 to 1952, my mother, grandmother, and I would go to the Riga seaside and rent a country house there. Over the years, we made many friends, establishing close ties with Riga. The situation in Riga was quite different from that in Leningrad: many people knew Yiddish and spoke it openly on the streets; there was nothing unusual in this. It was there that I heard for the first time of the possibility of going to Israel, however theoretical that concept might have been.

Baltic Jews were not assimilated to the same extent as Jews in Russia, and they retained their Jewishness. Moreover, in the late 1950s, it was possible for Jews who had Polish citizenship before the war to leave the Soviet Union. As many Jews utilized this opportunity and went through Poland to Israel and other countries, there was always a continuous stream of movement, albeit a weak one. For example, my close friend, Moshe Glaser, repatriated to Israel in 1971; his parents left even earlier, back in the mid-1960s.

I remember a conversation between two Jews that I accidentally overheard on the street. One asked, "Well, what's the score?" And the other said, "Nine to two." Initially, I thought that it was a hockey or soccer score, but it turned out that this meant that nine Jews had received exit visas to leave the country and two had been refused. Who knows, perhaps it was vice versa; nine refusals versus two exit visas.

"Enemy" radio "voices" (BBC, Deutsche Welle, The Voice of America, Radio Liberty) exerted a great influence on us, as they did on many other Soviet Jews; they were usually jammed, but late at night I sometimes managed to hear something.

The turning point for us was the so-called "Hijackers' Trial" in Leningrad. In June 1970, two groups of Jews from Riga and Leningrad made a desperate attempt to hijack a plane on an internal flight from Leningrad to Petrozavodsk in order to fly to Sweden and then to Israel from there. KGB agents seized them at the airfield before they succeeded in boarding, and the Soviet court, the self-styled "most impartial in the world," sentenced two of the hijackers to death by firing squad. Fortunately, the death sentences were commuted to fifteen years maximum-security imprisonment.

## Refusal

I must confess that at that time, Solzhenitsyn was still closer to me than Ben-Gurion. We finally decided to leave for Israel. As both of us worked in secret organizations, we realized that at the time, obtaining permission to leave the country was completely unrealistic. However, there was always the hope that the "iron curtain" separating the Soviet Union from the free world would eventually fall, and we wanted to be ready for that.

In 1972, I had already passed the exams required for my PhD degree, but in August, I told my supervisor that I was not going to continue scientific work and would not be writing my thesis. Then Ida and I retired from our "secret" organizations.

Soviet rulers could not permit their citizens to leave the country for nationalist or ideological reasons; this might cast a shadow on the country of "victorious socialism." With very few exceptions, people could leave only for so-called "reunification of dispersed families." It did not matter whether you really had relatives abroad or not. Therefore, everybody who wanted to leave had to make up a fictitious aunt or uncle who lived in Israel; the officials pretended to believe those legends. Such were the rules of the game.

Even this game had various restrictions and regulations that were aimed at making the process of reunification as difficult as possible. In 1972, the Soviet government imposed a very heavy ransom on people with higher education who wanted to leave for Israel. We, of course, did not have such large sums of money at the time. In addition, all repatriates were forcibly deprived of Soviet citizenship and had to pay a substantial sum of money for this honor.

First, it was necessary to find a job, any job. I could not ask my friends to help me because it would be immoral to hide our plans from them, but not to hide them would be impossible and who would be able help if they knew of our plans to leave? I therefore applied to a taxi driving school, where they even gave me a scholarship. While attending the driving school, I also worked part-time in a commission for the assessment of equipment in a vocational school, a temporary job my Uncle Isaac helped me find. Ida also found a similar job in another vocational school.

The head of the commission was one Simon Pitkin, an old Bolshevik and a Jew. In his youth, he had a beautiful voice and, before the revolution, sang at Jewish weddings in Ukraine. Later he became a Bolshevik, which was the sole reason that he was accepted to the Conservatory of Music. There he fell in love with a beautiful girl from a disenfranchised family. Pitkin was summoned to his party committee and given an ultimatum: "Either the girl or the conservatory." He chose the conservatory. However, not only did he not become a singer, he eventually went to work for the Cheka, which later became the NKVD first and then the KGB (the equivalent of the CIA) after that.

He told us that when he was the head of the "special" department in one of the Leningrad "secret" organizations, his bosses from the KGB used to order him to summon "so and so." He obeyed the order and this person would disappear forever. In this way, he summoned two hundred people; then he was taken as the 201st. He thought that this would be his end but at that time a "purge" of the entire staff of the KGB began; his former investigator was dismissed and the new one let Pitkin go free. Pitkin always bad-mouthed Israel, loudly and picturesquely. He sang wonderfully, however. We often heard him sing.

Working in the commission, I met Simcha Epstein. We quickly figured each other out as experienced conspirators. It turned out that he had a son in Israel, and that he himself would like to go there.

## A driver

After my stint at the driving school, I did not become a taxi driver but instead found a job as a truck driver in a company called Lengaz (The Natural Gas Company of the city of Leningrad). I decided that as a truck driver, there was less chance of having an accident than for a taxi driver, although the job paid less. In an old, rickety truck, I delivered materials needed to repair gas heaters and the milk rations for the office workers. As the job in this company was considered harmful, the workers received milk, and I also obtained some. I worked from eight in the morning until five so I simply did not have any time left for Zionism.

Our friends, who had paid for their education, and had thus received their exit visas, arranged an "invitation" for us from Israel, which arrived quickly. However, in order to apply for exit visas to Israel, we also needed a character reference from our former employers. I received mine without any problem from our house committee because I was unemployed at the time, but for Ida it was more complicated. She worked at a post office, and after requesting a character reference, was subjected to a full staff meeting, organized for the sole purpose of mocking and criticizing her. Ida justified her request by explaining her husband's desire to move to Israel to join his relatives. At that, everyone insistently tried to persuade her to divorce me, promising to find her a new husband, much better than her current Zionist one. To their surprise, Ida did not succumb to their persuasions.

We applied for our first exit visa in our district Department of Visas and Registration (OVIR) in May 1973. There were three of us: Ida, our son Misha, and myself. As we did not expect them to grant us permission to leave, we did not include my mother in the application in order not to complicate her life. After a wait of three months, the head of the OVIR, Colonel Bokov, told us that our request was rejected because of our previous classified jobs. That is how our life as refuseniks began.

As we became accustomed to our new status, we were invited by Grisha Goman, Josef Blikh, and others to go to a demonstration on December 24, 1973, to protest the harsh sentences given to the "hijackers"; it was the third anniversary of the first Leningrad trial. I did not dare to go at that time, fearing arrest. I had not yet got rid of the fear that our new situation aroused, but later, I started doing mental workouts, using autosuggestion. I constantly asked myself: "What could they possibly do to you, put you in a prison? That's it?" As soon as I got accustomed to that idea, I became a free man. In 1975, I finally got rid of fear. Over the years, I even began to get some kicks from all this surrealistic interaction with the KGB.

## *Elevator mechanic*

After receiving our first "refusal," I resigned from Lengaz and decided to seek employment through the Employment Bureau. Considering it immoral, I did not hide my plans or situation as a refusenik from my potential employers, and it was thus no wonder that nobody wanted to hire me.

One of my friends then helped me find a job as a residential elevator serviceman. My duties included testing the working condition of forty elevators in residential buildings and informing the dispatcher about all detected failures; that was it. Ida also technically started working there, but I actually performed all the work for her. The work was not very exacting and it paid mere pennies.

In the autumn of 1974, we decided to take a weeklong vacation in the Caucasus near Novy Afon (New Athos) on the Black Sea coast. We lived in a tent on the beach and cooked our food on a campfire. I made a deal with my fellow mechanic at work that he would do the entire job for us and we would pay him for his service.

As it turned out, we were already under the constant surveillance of the KGB, which monitored our every move. Our "deal" with my colleague was thus quickly exposed. Upon our return from vacation, we were summoned to the personnel office and were threatened with dismissal due to "absenteeism." I offered to resign instead, and in the end, they agreed. Apparently, it was not advantageous for them to have an extra case of misdemeanor on their books.

Immediately after that, I went to a similar "residential elevator service office" in another district, and they offered me a job. As it turned out, I took the place of the father-in-law of a Prisoner of Zion, Vladimir Mogilever, who had received permission to emigrate to Israel. Compared to my previous job, this one had a very convenient schedule: I was on duty for twenty-four hours in a small closet on the first floor of a fourteen-story building, and then, for three days, I was free.

As there was now more than enough time for moonlighting, I started giving private lessons in mathematics to high school students, and then, after learning a little Hebrew from our first teacher Benjamin Khaikin, I began to teach Hebrew myself (for the nominal price of one ruble per lesson per person). At the same time Ida, having mastered the technique of teaching English using the "pictographs" method developed by Rudolf Tenenbaum, began giving English lessons for the more realistic price of ten rubles per lesson per person.

All in all, it was enough for a decent living.

## Unemployed

I worked as an elevator mechanic until 1977, but then resigned from my work and decided to "tease" the Soviet authorities a little. By law, everybody in the former USSR had to be employed prior to leaving. People who were not working were arrested and jailed or exiled as "parasites." My game was to draw the enemy's fire upon myself and to see what happened.

Of course, I was not as fearless as it may seem at first sight. When I started this "game," I made a secret agreement with a fellow refusenik, a well-known mathematician, Professor Abram Kagan, who hired me as his secretary (fictitiously of course). Very few people knew about this contract, except myself, Abram, and the clerk in the financial department of the district executive committee.

Of course, we soon received a visit from the *druzhinniks* (a voluntary social organization in the Soviet Union, assisting the police in maintaining public order), who were sent by the police to check on my employment. I had always answered that I was working when asked, but only in court would I agree to disclose the name of my employer. The poor druzhinniks had no doubt that I was likely a drug addict or an alcoholic, as well as a wife abuser and they kept trying to persuade Ida to "tell on me."

## Work in a public bath

By 1981, it became clear that the KGB had no interest in arresting or jailing me, and I decided to start working for real again. At that time my fellow refuseniks, who were engineers, teachers, scientists, etc. by profession, as a rule made a living working as elevator mechanics, boiler room operators, and in other not very prestigious positions. It was necessary to hide the existence of a university diploma, because it was forbidden for the personnel departments to hire overqualified people.

My refusenik friends helped me obtain a job as a stoker in the natural gas boiler room in a public bathhouse. There were five of us on the team, headed by Lazar Kazakevich: Misha Gotz, Mark Budnyatsky (his wife Frieda was an accountant at the same bathhouse), Sasha Khodok, and myself. Naturally, all were Jewish refuseniks except for one: Sasha Khodok was a professional stoker, and even knew how to clean the boilers from inside. These boilers were by no means the latest development in technology as they were recycled from antiquated British steamboats.

We made our own schedule: a shift of almost twenty-four hours and then four days free. The members of the team held two positions simultaneously: as stoker and as operator. Officially, it was forbidden to receive two salaries, and we therefore listed our relatives for the positions of stokers; these relatives and friends needed no money but only a cover to avoid being imprisoned for "parasitism." Periodically, KGB agents visited the director of our baths, demanding that she dismiss all our team. However, our director, Zinaida Anufrievna Golanova (may God bless her memory), a decorated and distinguished member of the bath workers union, who had hardly finished elementary school, refused to bow to them. She always replied that as we never came to work drunk, had zero absenteeism, and our boilers never exploded, there was no reason to dismiss us.

An article called "Business of Slander" appeared in the local newspaper *Vecherny Leningrad* (Evening Leningrad). In this article, Lev Shapiro and I were accused of selling classified information to foreign anti-Soviet organizations. We supposedly possessed this information because we had previously worked in 'secret' enterprises. Zinaida Anufrievna was in shock, and from day to day, she was expecting my arrest. I tried to avoid distressing her with my presence, which was not very difficult because the boiler room was in a separate building, far from her office. She herself did not generally come to inspect us very often.

A month passed, and our director, seeing that I was still walking free, drew the correct conclusions. Namely, that the facts in the article were not confirmed. Therefore, when some time later, another local newspaper *Vecherny Leningrad* published a note about my "criminal links" with foreign emissaries, who came "to collect false and biased information in exchange for foreign second-hand junk," she did not react to this at all.

Then a different sort of event happened. A new night guard was hired at the public bathhouse. His name was Rosenberg, and his origin was either naturalized German or Estonian. One night when Sasha Khodok was on duty, Rosenberg, accompanied by another man, a welder who was doing some work for the baths, came into the boiler room, and together they gave Sasha a beating, telling him that they disliked Jews and explaining why they disliked them. In short, it was a common scandal for that time.

An urgent meeting of all bathhouse personnel was called. Even Comrade Portnoy, the general manager of the Leningrad City' Baths and Laundry came to this meeting. After Zinaida Anufrievna told the gathering about the night's incident, Rosenberg took the floor and explained, in simple terms, that his life had been ruined because of the Jews and that he was even expelled from the Party because of them. And here in this boiler room, people are working who are teaching the Jewish language! It cannot be tolerated. Portnoy took our side, saying that it was not a crime to learn your own language, and he himself regretted that he did not know the Jewish language.

It looked as though the meeting was going in the right direction and the act of hooliganism would be condemned. But no such luck. Rosenberg began to hint that he was there not of his free will, but that he was performing a task for a certain organization. I noticed that Portnoy paled: things were turning out bad, and I thought it was necessary to help the boss. I therefore explained that Rosenberg was apparently hinting here at the KGB, but that I suspected that it was just a case of megalomania because, up to now, when this organization purported to deal with me, they acted directly, without intermediaries. I also suggested that, as we could not work together with Rosenberg, it would be advisable to separate us. At this point, the meeting concluded.

Later, interestingly, Lazar Kazakevich collected some "undercover information" about this Rosenberg and found out that the authorities used him as a "decoy," like an informer in prison. Because of this, the criminal dons had a big grudge against him, and at the next one of Rosenberg's shifts, a group of fellows, whom Lazar had found somewhere, came to the bathhouse and started screaming, calling Rosenberg out and threatening to kill him. After that night, Rosenberg disappeared without a trace.

In the summer of 1984, an article appeared in a newspaper about a group of American tourists who had just checked into a Leningrad hotel. Two of them were later seen sliding into the dark carrying heavy objects.

The police, ever alert, tracked them down in an outlying neighborhood, where it became clear to them that the goods they carried were worth a lot of money. The tourists were, of course, unable to give a satisfactory explanation for their secret activities but the Soviet police soon worked out that this was all part of an international Zionist plot to create the "Jewish Problem" that the Soviet Jews were anxious to relay to the west. It appeared that various organizations in the west were encouraging this aim.

The authorities had also unearthed a figure well known in Zionist circles for his seditious activities.

This was A. Y. Taratuta, a former engineer, who changed his job in the field of astronomy for a position as a stoker in a bathhouse and laundry in order to make it easier to dress in the tattered toga of the persecuted and dispossessed. The last words are not accidentally in quotes. Judging from the contents of a failed broadcast, Taratuta, in addition to his dubious fame as "a fighter for the trampled rights" of the Jews, has more than a substantial income from the rat race of the Zionist scenarios.

Our country has been advocating for the broad development of international contacts and cooperation in all spheres—political, commercial, and cultural. However, there will always be a solid barrier to this created by the ideological saboteur.

## 3.

# Father Michael (Misha)

As difficult as our time in refusal was for us, it was even more difficult for our son Misha.

His story started during his years in the Leningrad middle school. In 1975, a decision had to be made about whether he would stay in the school that he had attended for several years, or be transferred to another one. His grades were pretty good, even though they weren't straight A's, and it was hard to know why they eventually did not let him stay in his first school. By that time, we had been refused exit visas and perhaps the school authorities knew that. This did not discourage him, and Misha applied to a school with intensive English language studies. Surprisingly, he was accepted, probably because of his good grades, and fortunately, at that time they still had openings. That school helped Misha develop his interest in the sciences. His situation was not bad, and he even escaped the necessity of being involved in the *Komsomol* (Young Communist League) organization that was a must for all Soviet teenagers.

His real problems started later when, in 1978, he graduated. We wanted him to go to Israel alone. However, he was not yet eighteen years old, and according to the rules, he would have to be accompanied by a relative. His grandmother agreed to accompany him and at once received permission to leave, but only without him. As a result, she did not go either.

That year, Misha applied to the college of his choice (he wanted to be an artist), but he failed to pass the drawing exam in spite of his manifest talent. The next year he applied to another college, one that he knew admitted Jews. By this time, it did not matter to Misha which college accepted him; he simply had to become a student because students in the Soviet Union were not drafted into the army. He worked very hard preparing for the exams and studied physics with the help of a private teacher, who was our friend and worked in this same college. Nevertheless, Misha failed the physics examination. We knew who was responsible for this, as they did not even try to make a secret of it. This person responded to one of his colleagues: "Had it not been I who failed him, it would have been done by somebody else."

After that, Misha managed to apply to another technical college, passed all his exams successfully, and was admitted to the night school. He did this just to confirm that he could. As he said, "I can pass exams when 'they' do not get in the way." However, there was no reason for him to study there because it would not protect him from being drafted into the army, and he was not interested in engineering. Instead, he attended the Technical School and for two years took courses in Showcase and Shop Window Design. The military draft office did not look for him for those two years; we had no explanation for his good luck.

In 1981, after graduating from the Technical School, he started working for a particular company. One day, a policeman came to our apartment and asked, "Why hasn't your son shown up at the local Military Draft Office?" We answered that we had not received any document for that. "But they called me and complained that he did not come," said the policeman. Of course, we understood that it was not the local draft office, but a "different" department from which the police office received this special request about Misha. We were sure that they knew he would not go to the army, which constituted sufficient reason for putting him in jail.

We decided that he had better make a preemptive move, so Misha went right away and visited the local Military Draft Office. There he found out that they were not looking for him at all. It even took them several hours to find his documents and direct him to the medical examination. Due to his poor vision, he was given a six-month deferment.

We thought that we had outwitted the KGB operatives, but we were wrong. A few days later, a policeman came and demanded that Misha once again come to the local draft office. Upon his arrival, the office clerk told him, "Yes, your draft was postponed, but the army needs an artist."

Now Misha was confronted by an uneasy choice: he could either be drafted or put in jail. He asked for advice from some people who had lived through a similar situation. One of them was Boris Kalendarev, and, on his advice, Misha chose the army because he knew that, in accordance with Soviet law, a person is still eligible to be drafted even after having served his time in prison. For example, once a young person named Simon Shnirman had refused to be drafted and spent two years in prison; then after he again refused to be drafted, he got an additional three years in prison. It was a very bad time for people who applied for exit visas.

Thus, Misha was drafted into the army and, as we had suspected, not for the position of an artist. First, he was sent to the Leningrad district, not too far away from the borders of Finland. A week later, he was summoned to the office of a KGB officer, a captain, who suggested that he inform on his fellow soldiers, for which cooperation he would be rewarded with benefits such as visiting his parents in Leningrad now and then. Misha asked the captain to give him his name. "Why?" asked the captain. "To tell this to my father, so that he could send a report about this to the appropriate department."

One week later, Misha was moved much further from the border and 80 miles from Leningrad to a village called Kamenka. To make his existence even more difficult, they kept moving him from one military camp to another, not allowing him to adjust to the local people and conditions. While he was not too far from Leningrad, we would travel there to see him almost every Sunday. The conditions there were terrible. "Bullying" amongst soldiers was a normal way of life in the army. There were not enough cots for the soldiers and they would steal overcoats and toothbrushes from each other.

After they discovered that he was an artist, they ordered Misha to design decor for the officers' club. In return, he was given permission to sleep there; this made his life a bit easier. However, the KGB kept their eyes on him and did not want him to have anything comparable to a comfortable life in the army. They therefore moved him, yet again ,to a new place.

Late one night in December 1981, we were on our way home when we saw a girl who turned out to be Misha's schoolmate; she and her father were waiting for us. They told us that Misha had called them (because our telephone has been disconnected as was usual when they wanted to make our lives more difficult) to inform us that he was moving to Archangelsk and would be passing through Leningrad.

His train was due to leave the Central Station in half an hour. We stopped the first car that appeared in the street and were at the station just five minutes before the train departed. We needed to find him in the train (which was more than 1,000 feet long!). We ran along the cars of the train and finally saw Misha looking for us from a window. We jumped into his car to embrace him and say goodbye; a minute later the train started moving to Archangelsk.

Misha later told us that on that day, he and the sergeant escorting him to his new posting had arrived in Leningrad early in the morning. The train to

Archangelsk was due later that same night. Misha tried to figure out how to tell us or call friends to inform us about his staying in Leningrad that day. He did not even have a two-*kopek* coin for a payphone. Meanwhile the escorting sergeant suggested that they spend time in a movie theater; Misha asked permission to visit the men's room, but he went to the theater manager instead and she allowed him to use her office telephone. It turned out, unfortunately, that none of his friends were at home at that moment. In the theater, he wrote the telephone number of one of his classmates on a piece of scrap paper and asked a girl next to him to call that number. She did and that is how, finally, the information about Misha reached us.

In Archangelsk, Misha joined a tank division, where he was assigned to plow snow. The commander of the unit could not understand what kind of misbehavior could have been the reason for his being sent there; for him Misha's case was very unusual. One month passed, and we were planning to visit him. We bought tickets for the train to Archangelsk, but, out of the blue, he was sent to a new place called Cherepovetsk. There was a construction unit there building a blast furnace for a huge metallurgical complex, so huge that the construction area had its own service train. Typically, the regime used free military labor for such construction, in particular, soldiers who could not be trusted to carry weapons. These soldiers were thus either former prisoners or men who had been sent to this place as an alternative to serving jail terms. Some were from the Caucasus and Soviet Central Asia. Thus, Misha, together with another young refusenik from Odessa, found himself placed in the midst of that company.

Gradually he adjusted to the way of life there. He began working as a painter and made the acquaintance of the Cherepovetsk City Chief Artist, who allowed him to assist in preparing big information stands with posters decorating the city. He and a fellow soldier were assigned to paint some propaganda plaques to decorate the blast furnace still under construction. They were given a separate room at the plant's main office in which to work and a special pass allowing them to leave there and walk, only by one particular path, on their way to the construction area and back. Misha spent evenings in a night school instead of wasting time in the barracks and eventually he graduated and got his second diploma consisting of all A's.

The entrance to the plant's construction area was not restricted to the public and we could visit him at any time. When Misha got leave for a day or two, we all usually came and stayed together in a hotel. It would take us one night on the train to reach Vologda from Leningrad. Sometimes we arrived early in the morning when Misha was at work. We would come to his work place and spend the whole day with him because he could not take time off. We would take the train back in the evening and would be back in Leningrad by morning. We brought him groceries and a small immersion heater for boiling water.

The KGB never left him alone. The soldiers from Misha's unit were called to the office of the captain responsible for political propaganda and asked to report on Misha's behavior and specifically to pay attention while they were watching the TV news. When these soldiers returned from the captain's office, they told Misha all about the conversation. They considered Misha to be their friend and tried to find a way to fool the captain. One day another officer approached Misha and said, "You should be careful when you write your letters home because they are read. And remember, I never told you anything."

Two years passed. It was the time for Misha's demobilization from the army. This usually took place in the USSR in September (they called it the "early discharge order"), and, of course, everyone wanted to go home as early as possible. At the commander's discretion, demobilization could take place later, on December 31.

At that time, Misha was assigned a special task: to decorate a so-called "Lenin's Room." He finished the job on time but still was not included in the list of soldiers being discharged from the army. This clearly indicated that something "fishy" was going on. Misha told us what was happening and we went to see his chief officer. We asked the officer the date of Misha's demobilization and he said that he didn't know anything about the "early discharge order" we referred to, and that Misha would be discharged from the army, in accordance with the existing regulations, by the December 31, 1983.

Following Misha's advice, we then went to see the commander of the Cherepovetsk Garrison: Vladimir Borisovich Braude. We waited for him for some time; he finally arrived, invited us into his office, and told his aide-de-camp not to disturb him for a while. He closed the door behind us and said, "My dears, I have been waiting for you for a long time." That perplexed us, but he continued, "Do you think that your son was sent to this city instead of to some distant, solitary place by chance? No way. When I saw the name of a Jewish boy on the list of the newly arrived soldiers, I decided to do something to help my people. And I placed him in this town."

After that, we told him our story of being refuseniks, and he said, "What I can tell you? I don't share your plans and ideas; that is your personal business, but I will try to help you with the problem of your son." He picked up the receiver and dialed the number of Misha's chief officer. "Do you remember that we are going to the baths this Tuesday? And by the way, the parents of that soldier are here. I don't remember his name, yes, Taratuta. We have to send him home today together with his parents. What captain are you talking about? Nobody told me anything about that, and I don't know any captain! Did you understand me? He has to go home today!"

The time was 4:00 p.m. Misha had to return all his military belongings and obtain the necessary documents. We rushed to all the required offices and after Braude's call, all the offices were open, with the personnel waiting for us. Thus, the obligatory procedure was completed in a speedy manner; Misha went home with us on the same day, November 16 1983.

When Misha was finally given permission to leave the country, he wanted to see and thank Braude. He took a bottle of cognac and went to his apartment. Unfortunately, he was not home at the time. Half a year later we, too, received permission to leave the Soviet Union, and I called the colonel to say good-bye. The voice on the other end of the line sounded somehow different. To my question what had happened, he said, "You probably won't want to see me when you hear my story."

Because our apartment was empty due to our upcoming departure, we arranged a meeting with him in a café. The former colonel told us that approximately a year earlier, he had been arrested. A major in his division wrote a report accusing him of corruption and stealing army property. They searched him but did not find anything to prove the accusation. Nevertheless, he was arrested. Fortunately for him, all this happened in the liberal era. Eleven months later, he was brought to court and sentenced to eleven months in prison, exactly equal to the time he had so far spent in jail. However, once he had a criminal record, he was stripped of his pension and Communist Party membership. We would have liked to help him, but our time in the USSR was running out quickly: in two weeks, we had to depart the country. We lost track of him for some time. Later on, we sent him some shoes from Israel for his children.

After he was released from the army, Misha decided again to try to attend college. According to Soviet regulations, a person who has served in the army enjoys the privilege of being accepted to a college without the required examinations, in particular, if the person had completed university preparatory courses. Misha wanted to study architecture and passed the university preparatory courses. He was the best student in the drawing class. Nevertheless, he was given a D grade in the drawing exam. When he was leaving the examination room in frustration, a co-student of his, who was the leader of the *Komsomol* (Young Communist) group there, approached him and said, "Don't be upset. Our teacher told us that in any event you wouldn't have been allowed to study with us at the university."

In August 1987, shortly after his arrival in Israel, Misha, along with his first art teacher, Eugene Abeshaus, went to the United States. Jewish organizations helped them organize a traveling exhibition across America, once again to draw attention to the plight of Soviet Jewry and to our fate in particular. On his return, he held a solo exhibition in Tel Aviv, and at the end of 1989, he moved to the United States and married a childhood friend.

# 4.

# Hebrew

In the 1960s, in Leningrad, the second largest and most important city in the USSR, "the cradle of the revolution," as it was called, the political atmosphere was more rigid than it was in Moscow. The local authorities sought the capital's approval for every action they undertook and thought that overdoing things was better than overlooking them. Many Jews were assimilated and tried to pursue careers in certain fields of science, art and industry, in which they were tolerated, by trying to hide their Jewish origin whenever possible. They had certainly heard about the state of Israel, but before the June 1967 Six-Day War, it did not affect them very much.

However, the underground Zionist circles in Leningrad were already active, led by David Chernoglaz, Vladimir Mogilever, Hillel Butman and Solomon Dresner, organizing the first home 'ulpan,' a course where Hebrew was taught. (Teaching and learning Hebrew was ostensibly permitted, like teaching any other language, but a Hebrew teacher could always be charged with Zionist propaganda and therefore, teaching Hebrew was practically illegal). After the Six-Day War, some activists began to seek permission to emigrate from the USSR to Israel. These activities became known to wider circles in 1970 with the arrest of "the airplane hijackers" and the authorities' campaign against them and other Zionists. Thus, in Leningrad, Zionist activities were suppressed for some time, but the emigration of Jews began. A network of ulpanim arose in the city.

The teachers were either elderly Jews from the Baltic Republics who had learned Hebrew before the Soviet occupation of 1940, or young people who had learned at least the first part of the Hebrew textbook *Elef milim*[5] (*A Thousand Words*).

---

[5] The first Hebrew textbook was called *Elef milim* (*A Thousand Words* in Hebrew), photocopies from which were circulated in Zionist circles for teaching purposes from the end of the 1960s.—*Editor's note.*

Ida and I started learning Hebrew in 1972, even before we applied to leave for Israel. Among our first teachers was Benjamin Khaikin (now living in Israel), a native of Riga. After several persistent attempts to talk him into teaching us, he finally agreed to do so. The lessons took place at his apartment. Among Khaikin's students were future Hebrew teachers, including Lev Furman, who later contributed greatly to establishing the network of *ulpanim* (classes for studying Hebrew) in the city, and our friend Eugene Abeshaus, a painter. There were eight students in the group who learned Hebrew using homemade copies of *Elef milim*.

We studied with Khaikin for two years before we started teaching Hebrew ourselves. It was Abeshaus who begged me to turn my hand to teaching—not because I had mastered the language so well but because of the dire shortage of teachers. The principle was simple: you learned three lessons and passed on your knowledge to the next person.

Among my first students were my son Misha and my cousin Tolya Epstein with his wife Clara; all in all we had ten to eleven people. Classes were held in our home. Some of the students dropped out before finishing the first part of the textbook, but the most steadfast (my cousin, for example) took up teaching afterwards.

By that time Ida, who had been educated as a translator from English, had learned a technique of teaching spoken English known as "the picture (stick man) method." This method had been invented (or improved) by Rudolph Tennenbaum. The results were fantastic. I also studied with him for two months. This technique appealed to me so much that I decided, my poor Hebrew notwithstanding (this is no fake modesty—I'm not very good at learning languages; I still can't claim I know good Hebrew; my former students outstripped me long ago), to produce a similar textbook for teaching Hebrew. I actually used this textbook for teaching until a very good primer called *Habet u-Shma* (*Look and Listen*) reached us.

My former students who later became Hebrew teachers included Anatoly Epstein, Boris Granovsky, Nelly Shpeizman, Lena Keis-Kuna, and Grisha Dikker. Eventually Ida also started teaching Hebrew to a group of elderly Jews. In 1976, in anticipation of the forthcoming International Symposium on Jewish Culture, Ida and I wrote a paper on teaching Hebrew with Tennenbaum's method. However, this paper, alongside with some other papers, never reached the Symposium because the authorities did everything in their power to prevent this "Zionist ganging-up" from taking place.

As an illustration of lessons in our *ulpan* (classes for studying Hebrew), I present to you a short essay written by one of my students:

## How I studied Hebrew

### The Reminiscences of Leonid Fridkin

I remember very well how in 1982, I began to study Hebrew in the illegal ulpan of Aba Taratuta. Now (in retrospect), I realize that his knowledge of Hebrew was not quite perfect, but at the time, we thought he was a great expert. Initially the group was fairly large, but over time, many pupils dropped out. The core group consisted of Grisha Geyshis, Grisha Dikker, Boris Vainerman, Ida, Aba's wife, and me. Occasionally the wives of both Gregory and Boris would also join, as well as the artist Yuri Brusovani.

We had one lesson a week at Aba's apartment in Kosmonavtov Prospekt in Leningrad. Aba provided books and cassettes and gave us Zionist literature in Russian and English, and supported us by his unfailing optimism, despite being a longtime refusenik.

Sometimes visitors from abroad would come to our lessons, and one day Igor Guberman appeared when he returned home after his imprisonment. From time to time, other well-known refuseniks also visited us. The atmosphere was calm and joyful, although we knew that we were under constant surveillance by the KGB.

Our studies lasted for some years, or rather seasons, from November to May. At the end of our courses, Aba handed us certificates attesting to the successful completion of the year, filling them out in Hebrew. We even had a graduation party; Ida prepared food, and we came with our wives, bringing liquor and something tasty. When sitting together, we forgot about how, when, and where we lived. Aba arranged a Passover Seder for us, and not only for us. The table was always adorned with a bottle of kosher wine from Israel. What united and obsessed us was the desire to leave the Soviet Union and make aliya to Israel as soon as possible. At last, that came true in 1987–1989. None of us ever considered going to any other destination.

Now I want to say a few words about the Russian wives of Grisha Dikker and Boris Vainerman, and many others who have linked their lives to Jewish activists and refuseniks. Their lives were much more difficult than for Jews. Their families could not understand their daughters' husbands' desire to immigrate to Israel. This often generated conflicts, even to the point of severing relations with parents and other family members, but they remained loyal to, and supportive of, their Jewish husbands.

Now we, all graduates of Aba Taratuta's ulpan, have been in Israel for more than twenty years. Some of us have aged; others have grown up. There were all kinds of problems, but none of us regrets the decision to come to Israel. It was the right decision. Every five years we meet to celebrate this event, the most recent time was in 2012, the twentieth anniversary of our aliya to Israel

# 5.

# Samizdat

I applied myself to working on *samizdat* ("self-publishing" in Russian, in circumvention of the censorship, which meant typing or photographing the materials needed) when I started teaching Hebrew in 1974. We were in dire need of textbooks and had to duplicate them by photographing every page of the textbook and then printing the pictures at home from film. Some students were able to make their own copies, but the overwhelming majority relied on their teacher, that is, on me. The late Yuri Shpeizman helped me a lot when he found some reliable photographers who could be entrusted with this work. I made it a point never to get to know them; in this way, even if I was arrested and was tortured, I would not have been able to inform on them.

Apart from textbooks, Yuri and I made copies of books, mostly from the *Biblioteka Aliyah* (Aliyah Library) series. Tourists from overseas brought books, and we photographed them, page by page, keeping the films. Gradually the films piled up and formed an archive that had to be stored somewhere. I asked my friend Sergey Rotfeld (now a resident of Jerusalem) to find a hiding place for this collection of films. He agreed and placed it in his own dacha (summer house) near Leningrad. When Yuri and I needed a film, he would fetch it from there.

We distributed our copied books in *ulpanim*, and not only in Leningrad. The samizdat books were sent to Moscow, to Yosif Begun, Victor Fulmakht and others, as well as to Riga, Vilnius, and even Birobidzhan.

In the summer of 1985, while I was there with a geological expedition (I wanted to see the *taiga* at the expense of the authorities), I met the warden of the local synagogue, which was the only one in use at that time in Siberia. For several years, we bartered with the congregation: we sent prayer books, *tefillin* (phylacteries) and *mezuzot* (doorpost signs) to Irkutsk, and they sent us matzot and Jewish calendars of their own making.

Duplicating *samizdat* via typewriter was the task of Vladimir Ilyich Dragunsky, a former associate professor of Marxism–Leninism. Apart from the two aforementioned journals, we duplicated some *samizdat* collections that I found interesting. The late Zhenya Matskin found a typist. I never saw her, either, and only met her when Zhenya was about to leave for the United States.

Thus, we had two ways of duplicating *samizdat* materials: printing photos and typing the material. Both were "kosher" from the point of view of Soviet legislation, and that goes without saying, that the authorities in charge did not consider the duplicated reading matter as anti-Soviet material. As to more advanced copying machines (Xerox, etc.), they were out of reach for the man in the street, while in offices they were kept locked in special rooms. In order to print a certain number of copies of any office document, one had to obtain a special permit from "the first department," where KGB people worked. Placing a private order with a state-owned print shop (other print shops did not exist in the USSR) was something you could not even dream of. First, print shops did not accept orders from private persons, and secondly, the censor's permission was obligatory, not only for any newspaper or magazine issue, but also for any flyer or even a matchbox sticker.

We were well acquainted with Victor Brailovsky and the late Yuri Gelfand and provided materials for the *samizdat* magazine *Evrei v SSSR* (Jews in the USSR). Ida translated entire chapters from the English of Elie Wiesel's book *Night*, and they were also published in the magazine. Igor Raikhlin wrote an article on the origin of the word *evrei* (Jews) for that magazine.

When we were in Tashkent, we became acquainted with a historian, Roman Ravich (he later tragically died in Israel), who wrote Uzbek history in the daytime and worked on Jewish subjects at night. He published (under a pen name) two articles in *Jews in the USSR*: on Karl Marx's antisemitism and on the antisemitism of Friedrich Engels.

Beginning in 1982, the *samizdat* journal *Leningrad Jewish Almanac* (LEA) started appearing in Leningrad, edited first by Yuri Kolker, Edward Erlikh, Gregory Wasserman, and Yakov Gorodetsky, and then by Michael Beizer and Shimon Frumkin. My job was to duplicate and distribute it.

One day we came across an English collection of essays called something like "Anti-Semitism, A Concise History of Anti-Semitism from Ancient Times to Our Day." We thought it was an interesting book, so the whole of our skiing-outings, bathhouse-visits, and workers refusenik groups set to work translating this book into Russian. Unfortunately, this translation was later lost forever.

# 6.
# Demonstrations, 1974

This 1974 demonstration was dedicated to the fifth anniversary of the severe sentences passed in December 1970 on those involved in the first "hijack plot" trial in Leningrad. In Moscow, it was organized by Moscow refuseniks.

In Leningrad, Israel Varnavitsky was responsible for the undertaking, He had hoped to fly to Moscow but the KGB operatives took his name off the flight list when he registered for a ticket at the airport. In addition, several of our friends were detained on the basis of the standard charge—violation of public order.

Six of us, refuseniks from the "northern group" of Leningrad, Eugene Abeshaus (now in Israel), Leonid Lotvin (now in the U.S.), Viktor Savitsky (now in the U.S.), Michael Bargman (now in the U.S.), and Valentin Stanislavsky (now in Australia) assembled at what was then my work place, an elevator maintenance attendants' room. After a short discussion, we decided to sneak out in a roundabout way via Novgorod. A day prior to the demonstration, we dressed in our warmest clothes (in case we were caught and detained) and met at Moskovsky railway station. We took two cabs and in two hours reached Novgorod, from where we took a night train to Moscow.

We reached Moscow at about 8:00 a.m. and decided to split into couples in order to avoid drawing attention to ourselves and to meet at the subway station, which we failed to do because we had not taken into consideration that there were two entrances to the subway at Leningrad station. Two of our pairs managed to re-unite after fifty minutes of wandering in the numerous underground passages and escalators, but the third pair had completely disappeared.

As there was plenty of time left before the scheduled beginning of the demonstration (noon), we decided to call Ilya Essas, one of the main organizers, to inform him of our arrival. This was necessary; first, in case we were arrested, and second, in order to make contact with the friends whom we had lost as they also had Essas's phone number. We started speaking to Essas in Hebrew, but then, to make sure that he understood, repeated everything in Russian.

On the way to the Supreme Soviet Presidium's reception room, we happened on our "lost" friends, so we all filed into the building together past a line of policemen and some plainclothes officers. A large number of participants assembled in the spacious reception hall in order to sign a letter of protest against the unjust sentence for those involved in the "highjack plot." Another Leningrader joined us there, Alexander Chertin, who had come to Moscow several days earlier.

Three hundred signatures were collected, with Alexander Lunts organizing the signing and the presentation of the letters; he handed them in at the document reception counters for the USSR Soviet Presidium and for the RSFSR Supreme Soviet Presidium. After that, Lunts invited the whole group to his apartment for a meeting. There were no refreshments there because the Lunts family was on a hunger strike, in addition to participating in the demonstration.

The return trip to Leningrad was uneventful. We took a day train and were met at the station by a large crowd of friends and relatives.

# 7.

# The Phone

We received our first refusal in August 1973, and in February 1974, our phone was disconnected for the first time, without warning. As it turned out, it remained disconnected for two years. At the district phone office, it was explained to me that, "it is technically impossible to reactivate the phone."

While disconnecting a phone was a common method of punishing refuseniks for "bad behavior," as the government saw it, in our case, it went like this. We were acquainted with the mathematicians Lena and Vladimir Oliker, who, in turn, were familiar with the famous ballet star Valery Panov, who was also a refusenik. The Panovs had good connections with foreigners, but their phone, as with the Olikers' phone, was disconnected. The Olikers, without our agreement, gave our phone number to the Panovs, who distributed it among their foreign friends.

Inevitably, foreign correspondents from newspapers and news agencies accredited in Moscow, as well as various activists from abroad, started calling us. All of them were of course interested in the situation of the Panov family, who were being denied permission to leave the Soviet Union. Once we came home and Misha asked us, "Who is Reuters?" This, it seems, was the initial reason our phone was disconnected.

Life without a phone involved overcoming various difficulties. Every morning I went to our nearest phone booth, taking with me a pocket full of two-cent coins (which was the price of one call from a payphone), and spent an hour there. Contributing to the problems of two-way communication with friends were additional obstacles.

Foreigners wanting to support Jewish refuseniks began arriving in Leningrad. Meeting with foreign guests always took place in one or another of our apartments. As we could not be reached by phone during that period, we had to be contacted some other way. Sometimes they used the phone belonging to Michael Conson, who lived in the house next door; sometimes they had to send us a telegram.

But we still kept in touch with foreigners. They would contact us by telegram, suggesting we go to the post office, where we could talk to them. Then we simplified that scheme by giving the phone number of our post office to foreign friends who could then call us directly, having agreed a pre-arranged time. While we waited for the calls, the postal officials treated us royally.

From 1975 on, we were phoned every two weeks from the United States by Lynn Singer, who headed the Long Island branch of the Union of Councils for Soviet Jews. She wanted to be informed of all of our affairs and was always ready to help. Lynn responded instantly to all of our requests.

Of course, the KGB, the following episode proved, bugged all these conversations. At her next visit to the post office, Ida, waiting for a call, went into the phone booth and heard an unfamiliar male voice on the phone saying, "Remove the client from the booth!" She hung up, went out, and asked the operator who that had been. The girl replied: "I do not know; the central telephone office employs only women."

In early 1976, our phone was reconnected, but in April 1976, it was cut off once again. The same pattern occurred the following year

Once, as I passed by the call center, an idea struck me: to register on the general waiting list for telephone installation. Normally, the waiting time for a phone would be several years, depending on the area of residence. We lived in a relatively prosperous new area but it took quite a long time until we got a postcard informing us that it was our turn to get a new phone. By then it was already somewhere in the mid-1980s. The new phone was connected, only to be disconnected again, for the fourth time, this time for "only" six months.

# 8.
# Seminars

## Seminars on Jewish culture

The first seminars I know about in Leningrad were organized by Felix Aranovich in 1974. He primarily delivered the lectures himself. The subjects of the lectures were Jewish tradition and history. There was also a cycle devoted to Jewish themes in the paintings of the Hermitage Museum art collection. Lectures were conducted on a regular basis and about ten to fifteen people attended. One of the lecturers was Alexander Boguslavsky. This seminar came to an end with the departure of Felix in 1978.

## Scientific Seminar

I was told by the Leningrad refusenik Irma Chernyak of the first time a scientific seminar was organized in Moscow by Yuli Kosharovsky. I liked the idea, but it took several years to implement it Leningrad.

By 1976, many scientists were forced to withdraw from research or teaching work after applying for repatriation to Israel. One of them was the mathematician Boris Granovsky (later a professor at the Technion in Haifa). A group of us—a dozen scientists—gathered at our apartment and decided to establish a Mathematics Seminar for scientist refuseniks. As I did not offer to become the leader (I did not consider myself a great scientist), Granovsky took on the task.

It is worth noting that this was in fact a very unhappy time. Few of our friends wanted to take any prestigious position in the community of refuseniks, primarily because it was unsafe. It was in some sense similar to being in a war situation: one is either on the front lines or at headquarters. For Boris Granovsky, his leadership was thus certainly an act of personal courage.

Lectures were held on Mondays in our apartment, in a room that measured 13 square yards. We had a folding blackboard and chalk; that was all we needed. The seminar was attended by anyone who was interested, not just mathematicians. Sometimes, scientists from Western countries gave the lectures. There were even a few speakers from Israel. (The USSR and Israel did not have diplomatic relations. Those who came from Israel were those who had dual citizenship.)

The seminar was attended by such well-known Leningrad scientists as Professors Abram Kagan and Alexander Zaezdny. Sometimes a scientist would come from Moscow, as did Professor Alec Ioffe. Gradually, the seminar reached beyond the purely mathematical. A scholar of the Pulkovo Astronomical Observatory delivered two lectures on cosmology.

Over time, we established a liaison with the president of the Haifa Technion, Professor Sasha Goldberg. The Technion granted our seminars official status, and Boris Granovsky periodically sent reports about our work, which I suspect that nobody read.

The authorities did not ignore our seminars. Once, during a regular meeting, militiamen came to check passports (the national identity document). Those who had no passports had to go to the volunteer militia department for identification. On another occasion, Boris Granovsky was grabbed on the street, pushed into a car and taken to "talk" to the KGB. He was almost in shock when he came to us after that.

In December 1976, someone from my former "secret" workplace sent for me to come to the Deputy General Manager on an issue related to my request for repatriation. In his office, two members of the KGB greeted me. At that time, an investigation was being conducted into the Sharansky case and I was threatened with arrest because of a possible leak of classified information to the West through the participants of the scientific seminar.

Later, the same KGB officers came to my work (I was working as an elevator mechanic) and offered to help me to get a professional job as a programmer in any of the organizations to which I had not been accepted. After a couple of months, they came again to find out why I had not used their help in finding employment. I had to explain to them that I did not accept gifts from the KGB. Leningrad activists basically avoided voluntary contacts with the KGB. We knew from our experience that the employees of that agency at times resorted to very sophisticated methods of dividing our ranks and they most certainly did not give "gifts" for nothing.

Soon I was summoned to the volunteer militia who alleged that they had received complaints from our neighbors about our having so many visitors. Apparently, this disturbed them. I asked to see the complaints and to have names named. This they (the militia) could not do and only showed me a report of our conversation. I promised the militia to continue behaving well and not to be less respectable than before.

After the departure of Boris Granovsky to Israel in 1979, Professor Abram Kagan headed the scientific seminar, and after a while, the meetings moved to his apartment. The seminar kept going for another four years.

## Legal Seminar

In the late 1970s, we hosted a legal seminar in our apartment. Its head, a former lawyer, Valery Segal, was the first who taught us not to fear the militia, explaining that the militia did not have as many rights as we imagined. Once a week, Segal answered refusenik phone calls at our house during the short period of time when we had a phone service. This was extremely important for everyone. We obtained a lot of useful information by studying the transcript of the interrogation of the refusenik, Arie Volvovsky.

Vladimir Albrecht, a well-known human rights activist in Moscow, gave two lectures to participants of the legal seminar. He was the author of the guidebook *How to behave at interrogations and during searches*. He arrived in Leningrad, despite a high fever, to teach us how to oppose the totalitarian system.

Vladimir Prestin, one of the leaders of the Soviet Jews' struggle for free repatriation, delivered an interesting lecture on how to avoid conflict. His advice was very useful, as the people gathered there were very different from each other in intellect and mentality and also in the degree of intimidation by the authorities. However, there were more conflicts among the Muscovites, where there were groups of refuseniks who held different views on the strategy and tactics of the movement in general. In Leningrad, the situation was calmer and more tolerant.

# 9.

# Unsanctioned exhibition

In 1976, a group of Leningrad artists decided to organize an unsanctioned exhibition at the wall of the Peter and Paul Fortress in memory of the artist Eugene Rukhin, who had been killed in a fire. There were rumors that the fire was not an accident, as Rukhin was well known in the West. One of the members of this exhibition was our close friend Eugene (Zhenya) Abeshaus. I, as God had cheated me of any artistic talent, enjoyed being with him.

Abeshaus understood perfectly well that the authorities would do everything to prevent the exhibition and try somehow to isolate its members.

The night before D-Day, Zhenya therefore left his house with a large bucket, as if he was emptying the trash. He then changed direction and came to our house on the bus with this bucket, which was, in fact, empty. He spent the night with us, and the next morning we went with him to the Peter and Paul Fortress.

At the same time, his wife, Natasha, with her little daughter Nika, went via the subway to the same destination. Natasha had a portrait of Rukhin painted by Abeshaus for the exhibition. When approaching the station, Natasha and her daughter were stopped by a policeman: "Entrance to the subway is forbidden with the picture!" Natasha tried to protest: "Yesterday it was allowed, but today it is not?!" In the end, however, they had to turn back and carry the portrait home.

Zhenya and I arrived safely at the arranged place and walked along the bridge leading to the fortress. In the middle of the bridge, two men in police uniforms came up to us and detained Zhenya. They did not pay any attention to me.

Later that morning, we learned that all the artists who had gathered to participate in the exhibition had been arrested. After spending three hours at a police station, they were released home. Not everyone was released, however. One of them, Kleverov, was accused of "having a natural resistance to authority." As a result, the authorities inflicted "injuries of medium severity" upon him, which is to say, they beat him up. Kleverov was threatened with several years in the camps.

The next day a group of artists organized themselves to go to the same police station and testify on behalf of Kleverov. Although we were not present during his detention and knew the details of this episode only from eyewitnesses, we also joined this group in order to be false witnesses. At 10:00 a.m., a dozen artists gathered at the entrance to the police station where Kleverov was detained. We were not allowed entry however and were told to return at 2:00 p.m. The policemen apparently hoped that no one would come for the second time from the other end of town. Indeed, as I recall, except for Zhenya and us, no one did come to the police station at two o'clock.

A police official interrogated me. Rather than take my testimony, he interested himself for an hour in my humble self: who was I, our family structure, our income, etc. At some point, he returned to my family, at which I exploded and flatly refused to continue the conversation. I said that I can testify to the innocence of Kleverov in the episode with the policeman and made sure it was entered in the record. When the interrogation ended, the investigator advised me not to take part in future in affairs that bear no relation to me.

I do not know whether there was any benefit from our testimony but after keeping Kleverov in custody for a few days, not only was he released, but was also told that he could apply for an Israeli visa. The authorities often used this technique to get rid of unwanted elements. Kleverov took advantage of this offer although in principle he had not been planning to emigrate.

We always tried to celebrate all the Jewish holidays, and as a rule, we did so at someone's home. Sometimes we tried to arrange our celebrations for a large number of participants, and in those cases, we tried to rent a place in a restaurant. A story about such a Pesach celebration in 1977 is described below by Tamara Kazakevich.

# 10.
# Pesach 1977

*Memories of Tamara Kazakevich, USA*

This tale is dedicated to the memory of those refuseniks, who died before receiving permission to leave the USSR.

Our Seder took place on April 2, 1977, in Leningrad. The refuseniks of Leningrad decided to get together to celebrate Passover. According to the lists of names kept in secret by the refuseniks themselves and sent to the West, there were about 150 Jewish families who had been refused permission to emigrate. These lists were, however, certainly incomplete as a lot of courage was needed in order to include one's name on such a list.

All refusals were issued on Fridays, so all those who were called to come to OVIR (the visa office) on a Friday would exit OVIR as refuseniks, and you needed courage to stop at the door on your way out because there was always a refusenik on duty to write down your name. That was an early stage of the Jewish emigration process, and the word "refusenik" itself had been coined only five years earlier.

We decided to celebrate the Seder together, as a group, in an organized way, as they always taught us in the Soviet Union! There were about one hundred people, all those who wanted to be together, to be among Jews for the Seder. We wanted to celebrate properly with matzot, with Jewish music, and even together with a Jewish couple from Canada!

We all contributed six rubles each, and thus collected six hundred rubles, enough to rent a whole cafeteria for the night. We made all the arrangements ahead of time and ordered the menu, all except for the matzot. A cafeteria, unlike a restaurant, does not have an orchestra, so we brought our own music there, consisting of a record player and records. We brought it all there well ahead of time, about 2:00 p.m., set it up, turned it on and tested the sound.

We were supposed to meet after 6:00 p.m. We could not tell the director of the cafeteria that we were going to celebrate Pesach. Instead, we told him that the purpose of our get-together was to celebrate the twenty-fifth wedding anniversary of one of the couples in our group. We knew that we were constantly being watched, with the authorities always ready to stop us if we attempted to do anything against their rules. They knew from experience what kind of things had already happened.

For example, once a group of fifteen Jews got on a train to Moscow, went to the lounge of the Presidium of the Supreme Soviet and sat down, on the day before the opening of the Party Congress, in order to present their complaints to Comrade Brezhnev personally. Another time, some rebellious types decided to stand right in front of OVIR on Zhelyabova Street holding a placard saying, "Let my family go to Israel!" Another did even better; he rushed into the office of the head of OVIR with a tape recorder in his hand and tried to record his conversation with the director.

The refuseniks of Leningrad were a mischievous group that behaved badly! They organized regular Hebrew classes, seminars in Jewish history, Jewish culture, in math and in law. Refuseniks who had been engineers or professors in colleges had lost their jobs when they applied to immigrate to Israel and were at that time jobless or working at chimney-plants or in bathhouses. They were particularly enthusiastic about conducting those seminars at the highest professional level. That is why we were constantly being watched.

Knowing all of that, we were very cautious in our preparation for Pesach. We never spoke about it on the phone. Nobody knew the address of the cafeteria where we were going to celebrate until the very last moment, when we all met at a subway station.

When we got off the subway train at Ploshchad Vosstania, Aba Taratuta and Anatoly Epstein gave each of us a colorful anniversary card with the address of the cafeteria and a quote from a famous story by Isaac Babel: "And never talk again of all this silliness."

Everything was arranged so thoroughly, and then everything almost fell through. When we arrived at the cafeteria, it was still not six. The doors were closed and outside about ten to twelve people from our group were already waiting. After 6:00 p.m., more and more people came to celebrate Pesach, but the doors remained closed. The doors were made of oak with glass in the top section. It was dark inside with no sign of any movement. It seemed as if we had all gathered in front of the wrong cafeteria. Snow began to fall, and it became very cold. We were all dressed up, not bundled up for stormy weather, as we had planned to walk fast from the subway station. But there we were, standing outside for more than half an hour. One young woman (now living in Jersey City) wearing a long evening dress, freezing and already completely frustrated began to knock on the glass, in order to make them open the doors. There was no reaction. She turned her back to the door and began to kick the door with her high heels. Some passers-by stopped to look at us. Hearing her bang on the door, somebody came out eventually and declared that, because of some technical glitch, the cafeteria would remain closed and our meeting would not take place.

Our crowd was growing; everybody was there. The crowd staring at us also grew bigger. Just imagine, one hundred Jews in front of a closed cafeteria. At last, Aba and Tolya joined us. They knocked on the door again. The same reply: "Something has broken in the kitchen; the cafeteria cannot be opened." "Don't worry, your money will be returned to you in a week."

We all knew that the orders to prevent our Pesach dinner came from the KGB. Maybe someone reported us, or they had figured it out themselves. Then we noticed that on each side of our group there were two policemen watching us, reporting to their supervisors from the scene with their walkie-talkies. The policemen, obviously not on their own initiative, but instructed to do so by their superiors, came closer and began to repeat loudly: "Citizen Jews, please disperse. The cafeteria is closed. Your meeting will not take place." Some people from our group began to worry and decided to leave, not expecting anything good to come from the whole affair.

Aba and Tolya were trying to convince everybody to stay; they were sure that we would find a way to do something. They got in a car and went to the Hotel Oktiabrskaia. The maître d'hotel asked, "How many people are there in your group?"

"About seventy-five," they said.

"No, we cannot let you in."

Quickly they drove to the Universal, another big restaurant on Nevsky Boulevard. Same question—same response—same result. Getting back in the car, Anatoly said: "Instead of seventy-five, I should have said twenty-five." However, of course, the restaurants had received instructions regarding the Jewish Pesach.

They drove back to where most of the group was still waiting, about seventy-five people, the most persistent, and the most stubborn. And there, leaning against the unwelcoming wall, were our guests from Canada, a newlywed couple, who had come to see their friends, a family of refuseniks. For them, this was their major experience of Soviet reality.

Finally, we found a restaurant and decided not to enter all at once but in small groups of four or five and take separate small tables.

There were very few people in the restaurant, but it soon got crowded. Our Jewish group, aspiring to celebrate Pesach, was noisy. We occupied about twenty tables. The waitresses looked pleased. They had already served dinner to two small groups of foreign tourists; one group from Hungary occupied four tables in one corner of the restaurant, the other group from East Germany had three tables. The orchestra played Soviet songs, a singer was singing. Several couples were dancing.

From that moment on, everything was marvelous and unforgettable. That very minute was the beginning of the first and only collective Seder of the refuseniks of Leningrad.

One of us walked up to the orchestra and asked them to play "Hava Nagila." Everyone knows that if you give musicians a ten-ruble note, they will play "Hava Nagila," even unauthorized, even if it is not on the program.

The Jewish tune began. About thirty refuseniks went to the middle of the room, and in a circle, holding each other's hands, danced and sang "Hava Nagila." Then all at once, all our twenty Jewish tables were lifted up and put together to form one long table. Aba and Anatoly brought in, and placed on the tables two big packages of matzot, while a blonde lady in a blue uniform, the maître d'hotel, ran back and forth along our long table, yelling, that it was against the rules to move tables in their restaurant, that nobody would wait on us, that there was no more food left, that we all had to get out. She realized that the Jews had played a trick on her and that she would most probably get a reprimand from her boss.

However, on what grounds could she throw us out? What did we do wrong? We were not hooligans, we were just having a good time, singing and dancing. Still, certain severe measures were taken at once. The orchestra stopped playing. The musicians gloomily began to put away their instruments.

"Why?" we asked. "We were told to leave," they answered. Well, we can sing without music, can we not? And we began to sing our Jewish songs, all the songs we knew. Somebody brought wine and apples. There we were all sitting together, singing, drinking wine, and eating matzot. The Hungarian delegation, sitting across the room, liked our idea. They also put their tables together and began to sing Hungarian songs. Their guide came over to our table and told us that we were setting a bad example to the foreign tourists and that we should stop singing. Instead, we sent our matzot over to the Hungarian tables as a sign of friendship and hospitality.

Because foreigners (Hungarians, Germans, and Canadians) were present in the restaurant, the maître d'hotel received new instructions, and waitresses brought us the hot dishes we had ordered, as well as wine. We went on singing Jewish songs. Then all of a sudden, we saw the musicians coming back with their instruments! They had been instructed to return and play Soviet songs. They were playing and the singer was singing "Vologda-gda-gda-gda-gda" so loudly, we could not hear each other anymore. It was past 10:00 p.m. We had had a great time; nothing could now spoil our evening, our Holy Day. Because we did it! We celebrated the Pesach of 1977 together. Not in a vulgar cafeteria, somewhere far from Nevsky Boulevard, all alone, unknown to the world. No, we celebrated our Pesach in one of the most fashionably chic restaurants in the center of Leningrad, across the square from the Moscow railroad station, among foreign guests. After all, the authorities had made fools of themselves when they prohibited our celebration in the cafeteria.

# 11.
# Warning

In early January 1978, we were approached on the street by a young man who handed me a summons to appear at the local KGB offices for a "conversation." An interesting question: how did he recognize us in such a public place? Apparently, our portraits in this particular KGB department were of quite good quality.

At the appointed time, I presented myself at the entrance office of the so-called "Big House" at 10 Kalyaeva Street, where the headquarters of the Leningrad KGB were located. I was given an entry pass and escorted into the main building to the office of investigator Kravtsov. It was he who had conducted "preventative talks" with me at the local police a month earlier.

Kravtsov sat me down at an iron table attached to the wall and offered to acquaint me with some relevant passages in one of the thick volumes he had with him marked "Secret." He indicated that it contained a list of prohibitions and regulations for workers from so-called classified organizations. One of the paragraphs, in particular, stated that employees with access to classified information have no right to communicate with foreigners. I reminded him that as I no longer worked in a classified organization, these rules could not apply to me. Unfortunately, he chose not to agree with me and responded that I remained the bearer of secret information and was therefore not allowed to communicate with foreigners.

Then the investigator showed me a secret decree of the Supreme Soviet of the USSR. As I recall, it was published on December 25, 1972 (it turns out there were such decrees!). It stated that a person who is issued a written "warning" about the ban on contact with foreigners could be prosecuted. According to the text, this decree pertained to "speculators" and "currency prostitutes," but it could easily be applied to our fellow refuseniks.

The investigator had already drawn up a protocol when he issued this "warning." He gave me the protocol to sign, which I refused to do, stating that I have a rule never to sign anything drawn up by the KGB. Moreover, I even attempted the ploy of switching from defense to attack, saying that I wanted right there and then to write a formal complaint to Yuri Andropov, the head of the Soviet KGB. Kravtsov replied to this, saying that my signature was actually not required; the signatures of two witnesses were sufficient to validate the protocol. He told me also that I could not appeal to the head of the KGB over the head of the KGB chief in Leningrad.

Nonetheless, he gave me a couple of sheets of paper, and I began to write about the illegal actions of KGB agents and their treatment of me, all of which revolved around my desire to establish permanent residency in Israel, to make *aliya*. I also wrote that KGB agents were interfering in my private life, visiting our home, and my place of work, etc. I wrote for such a long time that the investigator lost his patience. Fat Kravtsov with difficulty lumbered out from behind his huge desk to see just what I was writing. He expressed his displeasure upon seeing that the complaint was addressed directly to Andropov rather than the head of the Leningrad KGB. Nonetheless. My letter was accepted, and he let me go home.

I do not think that my complaint ever reached the chairman of the KGB. But the fact remains that, after I wrote my complaint, the members of this department ceased visiting my work and home. True, they found other ways to apply pressure on our family. But that's another story.

# 12.

# Visits to places of detention

## *To Mark Dymshits*

Our friend Lev Furman gave considerable help to the family of the pilot Mark Dymshits. This was after the first trial in the 1970 "Hijacking Trial," in which Dymshits received the death sentence, which was later commuted to fifteen years in high-security camps, thanks to Western governments' pressure on the Soviet government. Lev introduced us to Mark's wife, Alevtina, and before her departure to Israel, I accompanied her on the long-distance flight to the place of Mark's detention. She had received permission for a two-hour visit. I did not meet Mark on that occasion because only his wife was permitted to be with him.

After the departure of Alevtina, Ida and I decided to take care of Mark. (Later we also supported Volodya and Masha Slepak and Irina and Victor Brailovsky, when they were in exile). In December 1978, Boris Granovsky and I went for an "approved" visit with Mark.

We flew by plane to Sverdlovsk and then took a train to the station Vsesvyatskaya. This was during the middle of the Siberian winter and it was exceedingly cold! The train arrived at night but indoors; the little wooden building of the station was warm enough. We spent the night near a wood-burning stove at the railway station and in the morning went to the village where the forced labor camp was situated. When we told the woman at the front desk in the camp office that we had come to visit Dymshits, she pulled a surprised face and said that there was no prisoner there by this name.

It transpired that we were not in the right camp; the one we needed was five kilometers further from the village. Once a day there was a shuttle bus but, as we were told it was already too late, we went by foot. The forest road was very beautiful in the frost and the sun. We had not even gone a kilometer when the shuttle bus caught up with us and drove us to the place. The driver even refused to take any money.

Prior to our visit with Mark, there was a briefing. An officer with a Georgian surname explained to us what one is allowed to discuss with the prisoner during the visit and what is forbidden. He also told us that he had served in Leningrad and was there during the "airplane incident." He was particularly interested in the price of American jeans and, in general, how life was in Leningrad.

In the meeting room, there were two tables. Boris and I sat at one table, Mark at the other one, on the opposite wall. Shields made of transparent glass were installed on both tables. To talk to Mark we had to shout at the top of our voice above these obstacles. At another wall sat a woman warden who ensured that our conversation was "kosher." Right beside Mark stood an armed guard.

Dymshits looked like a well-balanced man, who had endured all the hardships of prison camp life with dignity. We tried not to touch upon any political subjects and the matron never interrupted us.

In 1979, a group of Jews was released from their places of detention. Among them were Anatoly Altman and Arye Khnokh from Riga. They were imprisoned in the same camp as Mark Dymshits. As all correspondence with Mark was opened and inspected by the camp authorities, I decided to go to Riga to learn about Mark at first hand. The meeting with the former prisoners was at the Zalmansons' place. Both of them confirmed the impression we got from our short visit with Mark at the camp.

## To Boris Kalendarev

Boris Kalendarev had been avoiding recruitment for a long time, moving to different places in the country, including Leningrad. Once he even made a trip to the Caucasus with Ida and myself. We visited Yerevan, Tbilisi, and the Black Sea Coast in Gudauta. However, in March 1980, he was arrested while riding on a city bus in Leningrad.

The lawyer to whom we went with Boris's parents happened to be Jewish. When we asked about payment, he replied that since the Romans invented money (for some reason he thought that it was them), nobody had invented a better system. His only functions consisted of visiting Boris in jail, handing him some sandwiches prepared by his parents, and then reporting back to them about Boris's health. It was obvious that he could not have had any impact on the court's decision. For the evasion of conscription, Boris Kalendarev was sentenced to two years in prison camp. The first time we visited him in a Leningrad jail it was not the famous Leningrad "Kresty," but another one, less known.

Boris was sent to serve his sentence in the Gulag in Kalmykia. In the fall of 1980, his father, Michael Abramovich, and I tried to visit him there. We flew by plane to Volgograd and then took a long taxi ride. As long as the road ran through the Volgograd region, everything was in order. The asphalt came to an end, however, and the car was not able to drive on the country road, because of mud from the rainfall. Crowds of people were looking for all-terrain vehicles or tractors to go further. It became clear that we would be stuck there for a very long time. Michael Abramovich suggested that we turn back for home, and I had to agree with him.

The next attempt we made was in the winter, when the roads were frozen. The small hotel in the village of Bolshoi Tsaryn near the prison camp was fully booked. As a war veteran, Michael Abramovich turned for help to the local authorities, and we were given the key to an empty trailer where local construction workers lived in summer. It was very cold outside—minus 25–30 degrees Celsius (minus 13–22 Fahrenheit), but inside we switched on an electric heater, which worked from a car battery, lay down on some cotton mattresses, and covered ourselves with other cotton mattresses. We spent the night there. In the morning, we both received permission for a two-day visit with Boris (I called myself his elder brother).

We talked with Boris all night long. He described the atmosphere in the camp where the majority of the inmates were locals who lived in the camp according to their own laws. Nevertheless, he managed to establish a communication channel with the outside, which allowed us later to smuggle some food into the camp. For Boris this was very important.

The third time I visited Boris together with Ida. At that time, he was already allowed to live outside the camp. He was in Elista, the capital of Kalmykia, and he enjoyed relative freedom. He worked as a construction worker and lived in a hostel, but twice a day he was obliged to report to the local authorities.

In 1981, when Misha reached conscription age, he went to see Boris in Elista to seek his advice on whether to go to prison or to serve in the army. Boris advised military service, and he was right; upon his own return to Leningrad after serving his term in full, he was threatened with conscription again. He had to take great pains to avoid it.

## To Alec (Roald) Zelichonok[6]

When Alec was serving his sentence in the camp in Ukhta (Autonomous Republic of Komi), I flew to visit him with his wife, Galina (Galya). I remember that it was terribly cold. We both had a few hours in which to visit with him. Although Alec was not in very good health, his spirits did not sink. We returned home on the same day.

Sometime later, Zelichonok was transferred to a prison camp in Central Asia (possibly for more warmth), but we did not know exactly which one. Ida and Galya flew to Alma Ata, the capital of Kazakhstan to search for him, but Alec was not there. They were told that he had been transferred to the city of Turkestan in Kazakhstan. They went there immediately, and the camp administration was so surprised when they showed up, as it was literally the day after the arrival of their new prisoner that Galya was given permission for a three-day visit.

On their way back, the heat was so oppressive, that the plane could not take off for a long time. The passengers, however, were kept in the cabin; apparently, the pilots were hoping that someone would melt, and it would be easier to take off and gain altitude!

I accompanied Galya for the next visit, which was granted for "good behavior" (a prisoner is given one visit every six months). We flew to Tashkent and from there drove 200 miles by taxi to the camp. We stopped at a hotel, and under the cover of night, went to one of the camp commanders, whom we bribed with gifts. He invited us to dinner, and at the table, we mentioned that the next day would be Alec's birthday. Hearing this, the host poured me half a glass of pure alcohol and proposed a toast to the health of the "newborn."

---

6    Roald (Alec) Zelichonok was arrested in 1985 and was sentenced to three years in prison under article 190-1 UK RSFSR (Production, storage and distribution of material containing clear fabrications discrediting the Soviet social and political system). He served his sentence in the Komi ASSR and in Kazakhstan and was released conditionally ahead of schedule in 1987.—*Editor's note.*

In such a situation, I could not refuse. The host himself did not drink at all because at that time he was being treated for alcoholism! The next day we received a brief two-hour meeting, after which we went back home.

My other trip to visit Zelichonok failed for rather prosaic reasons. Galya and I had already purchased plane tickets, and we were ready to go, but the eve of our departure was also our traditional "sauna day" that I did not want to miss. As I mentioned before, many refuseniks, myself included, found jobs in the boiler rooms at bathhouses. We used to gather in the baths, where Edward Markov worked, once a week on the day when the baths were closed to the public. We were there alone and the door was not locked. A thief climbed in and stole my bag with my plane tickets and passport. The problem with the tickets could have been solved, but you cannot fly without a passport. The passport was eventually tossed back, but it was too late, and Galya flew with Ilya Simovsky.

# 13.

# The Search

The doorbell rang early in the morning on April 10, 1980 in our apartment on Kosmonavtov Prospekt 27/1. When I asked, "Who's there?" a female voice answered, "A telegram for you!" I looked through the peephole and saw a young woman who was holding a sheet of paper in her hand. I opened the door and let her in. Immediately another nine men and women broke into the flat. This was a search.

> Search Warrant
> Public Prosecutor: Koloskov
> Investigator: Ponomaryov
> File 49608/13-80
> Legal grounds for the search—telegram from Moscow. (*This proved that there was some truth in what the "post office girl" had said.*)
> The bearer of this is empowered to carry out a search of A. Y. Taratuta's apartment and to question the aforementioned about the results of the search.
> Signed: Smirnov, Investigation Office Deputy Manager (Moscow)

I took this document in my hand in order to copy its contents and at that moment, I recalled that I had a list of not entirely "kosher" books and the people to whom I had lent them. An idea occurred to me: I would copy the search warrant on the other side of that same list and place it where it could easily be seen by everybody. The trick worked. The sheet of paper remained untouched where I had put it, and no one thought of checking what was written on the other side.

The people who searched our apartment were a certain Levanov, Moskovsky District of the Leningrad Public Prosecutor's Office investigator, his six assistants (who looked suspiciously like KGB men), and two female witnesses, one of whom lived in our building. The investigator demanded that I voluntarily hand in the anti-Soviet literature that I was keeping in my apartment. On hearing that there was none, they started to search.

They placed Ida and myself in separate rooms. One of the "aides," not the investigator, gave orders to everyone. From what they put aside, it became clear that what the "organs" considered anti-Soviet literature was any book that had even a single Hebrew letter in it, whether Hebrew or Yiddish. They included in this category, among others, a Yiddish calendar published by the Moscow Choral Synagogue and a Hebrew Bible with a Russian translation, published in 1902. I could not keep myself from asking: "Did they really start publishing anti-Soviet literature so long before the Soviets came into existence?" The answer I got from investigator Levanov was "You do crack some jokes, Aba Yakovlevich!" Then he added, "Don't worry, everything will be returned to you." (Naturally, nothing was returned.)

There was a washing machine in the room where they placed Ida, and everyone saw it as their duty to look for hidden criminal evidence in its insides. Next to it, under a chair, there was a big briefcase, tightly packed with Jewish *samizdat*. It was covered with some laundry that was hanging down from the chair, and no one thought of looking behind it. They asked whose coat was hanging on the peg. I said it was my son's and they did not examine it, which was lucky as in one of its pockets there was my telephone book with numerous Jewish activists' addresses and telephone numbers.

Now and then the "assistants" would ask the "boss" for advice. He decided what to confiscate and what to leave. For example, they did not take away E. Ginsburg's book *Journey into the Whirlwind* (Krutoi marshrut). Apparently, its subject matter did not lie within the specific interests of KGB's "Jewish" department. On the other hand, they put aside *The Gulag Archipelago* by Solzhenitsyn, which I did not find on the confiscated items list later. I thought it wise not to mention this fact. The "boss" handed the valuables (tape recorder, watch, etc.) to Ida after a check-up. It seemed as though he did not have much faith in his colleagues.

The search lasted four hours. I was presented with a written account of the whole process and with it a list of all the confiscated items.

These included:

- A Russian typewriter, made in Holland;

- An English typewriter, made in the U.S.;

- Personal letters;

- Hebrew books, dictionaries, telephone books; and

- Foreign-made audio cassettes with English and Hebrew lessons, and Jewish songs and my son's jazz cassettes—seventy in all.

All these things filled seven sealed bags.

It became clear later that the search and the interrogation that followed were connected with Victor Brailovsky's arrest in Moscow and the criminal charges leveled against him of publishing the *samizdat* magazine *Jews in the USSR* (*Yevrei v. SSSR*). We found out that several other searches had been carried out at the same time, in particular at Alexander Maryasin's apartment in Riga.

# 14.

# An Investigation at the Public Prosecutor's office

A couple of days later, I was summoned to an investigation at the District Prosecutor's Office by the same Investigator Levanov who had carried out the search. I wrote down his questions and my answers.

*Levanov's questions:*

1. Tell me about your family.

2. What do you know about the publishing of the *Jews in the USSR* journal?

3. Do you know Brailovsky?

4. Who distributed the magazine in Leningrad and Riga?

5. Have you seen issue No. 20?

6. Did Brailovsky bring the magazine to you during the years 1979–1980?

7. Do you know the publishers of the *Law and Reality* journal (*Zakon i deistvitelnost*) in Riga?

8. Where did you get the magazines *Tarbut* No. 6, 1976, and Nos. 8, 9, 1977, and to whom did you lend them? Are you aware of the fact that this magazine is a supplement to *Jews in the USSR*?

9. Do you know A. Maryasin, a resident of Riga?

10. What *samizdat* magazines, apart from *Tarbut, Law and Reality, Leaving for Israel* (*Vyezd v. Israel*), *Jurisdiction and Practice* (*Pravo i praktika*) do you know?

*My answers:*

1. I answered the first question.

To questions Nos. 2, 3, 4, 6, 7, and 9, I said that I had not been informed of the core facts concerning the case which I was being interrogated about; that they had failed to explain them to me and that I could not give evidence as a witness in a case, the basics of which were unknown to me.

To questions Nos. 5, 8, and 10, I answered that these questions were of a personal character and, in my opinion, they could not be relevant to the case about which I was being interrogated.

To conclude, I added, at the interrogator's request, "Had I been informed of the contents of the case, I would have been able to give more detailed evidence."

## 15.

# The Jewish Library

In 1981, Isaac Mikhailovich Furshtein, a man who had had a serious impact on refusenik intellectuals in the 1970s, left Leningrad to join his daughter in the United States. Throughout his adult life, Isaac Mikhailovich had collected books, pamphlets, and magazines on Jewish subjects in Russian. Most of these publications had been printed before the Bolshevik revolution and during the first years of the Soviet regime. The result was an outstanding library, numbering about 800 items. Among his books were the collected works of Dubnov and Gessen, the *Jewish Encyclopedia* in seventeen volumes, the magazines *Voskhod* (Sunrise), *Evreiskaya Mysl* (Jewish Thought), and others.

Furshtein allowed practically everyone to use this library. Among its constant readers were Michael Beizer, Grisha Wasserman, Sasha Genusov, and many other Leningrad activists. I was on very good terms with Isaac Mikhailovich, his wife, and his daughter. Shortly before leaving the country, Furshtein suggested that I buy his library for our refusenik "community." He prepared a list of books and priced each of them. The total came to 10,000 rubles. We did not have that much money, so I arranged with Lynn Singer (of the Long Island Committee) that, on Furshtein's arrival in the US, she would give him three thousand dollars.

For two reasons it was definitely impossible to keep this library at our apartment. First, there was no room for it: our apartment had only two rooms, with a total living space of 27 square meters. Secondly, after the recent search it was clearly unsafe for the library to be in our apartment. Eventually, I found two wonderful young women, Lena Romanovsky and Tanya Makushkina, who agreed to take care of the library.

Lena's husband Daniel had an unoccupied room in Marata Street to which we moved most of the books. Lena's library was given a code name "GPB" (*gosudarstvennaya publichnaya biblioteka*—State Public Library), and it was a lending library, open to all readers. The rarer and more valuable books were dubbed "BAN" (*biblioteka akademii nauk*—the Library of the Academy of Sciences) and could be reached through Tanya, who would bring these books from their secret hiding place, at Misha Tserelson's apartment, on request.

It was my job to give the books a face-lift as some of them, as the saying goes, were ready to bite the dust. For this purpose, I recruited a friend who could bind books almost professionally. I would bring him some five books at a time, and in about a year and a half, he finished this work at a minimal cost.

Now and then, our library would get a fresh influx of books. When Sara and Daniel Fradkin were leaving for Israel, I bought another set of the *Jewish Encyclopedia* from them. I then obtained a whole collection of books on Jewish subjects from another emigrant, Leonid Belotserkovsky. As a result, we had many second copies, which I gave to Yosif Begun. As far as I know, these books gave a start to the Moscow Jewish library founded by Colonel Yuri Sokol. He came to visit us from Moscow some time before our leaving for Israel.

After receiving permission to leave for Israel, I transmitted all my archives, passwords, and clandestine rendezvous addresses, together with the communal funds, to Boris Kelman. (Boris and his wife Dr. Alla Kelman later immigrated to California.) He was also in charge of our Jewish library, which seems to have ended up at the Leningrad Kirov Palace of Culture where the "Jewish Cultural Centre" has been housed since 1989.

# 16.

# Interrogation at the KGB, 1982

We were well acquainted with Valery Repin, a human rights activist who was in charge of the Leningrad branch of the "Solzhenitsyn Foundation." The Foundation provided material support, helped political prisoners' families with money, and collected information on conditions in the forced labor camps. I helped him with whatever I could (for instance, I introduced him to the trusted man in whose place he was then able to keep his archive), but I did not participate in joint actions with dissidents because I felt that our goals were different.

At the beginning of the 1980s, Repin was arrested, and I was summoned for an investigation together with other witnesses. A long talk with the investigator preceded the interrogation. The talk centered on a wide range of subjects, including the international situation. Then the investigator proceeded to the interrogation proper. When I was outside, I wrote down everything that I remembered of the proceedings while it was still fresh in my memory.

> **Question:** Do you know Valery Repin?
> **Answer:** I refuse to give evidence; I see this interrogation as a means of pressuring me because of my desire to leave for Israel.
> **Question:** It has been explained to you that your desire to leave for Israel has nothing to do with Repin's case; you are therefore requested to clarify your reasons for refusing to give evidence.
> **Answer:** In 1973, I submitted documents for leaving, for permanent residence in Israel, and in the same year, I was denied the right to leave, without, in my opinion, sufficient grounds.

Since then the authorities' permanent pressure on me has included:

- Multiple unexpected raids on my apartment by the police and Civil Guard, ostensibly for passport regime control;

- A search of my apartment by the Moskovsky District of the Leningrad Public Prosecutor's Office's people in connection with a legal case unknown to me, on April 14, 1980, in the course of which my personal correspondence, Hebrew books, dictionaries, notebooks, and telephone books were confiscated. They have not been returned to me in spite of my repeated requests;

- Disconnecting my home telephone three times for long periods of time, without any explanation of the reasons for this;

- Myself and my wife being repeatedly summoned for interrogations to the Prosecutor's Office in connection with fake criminal cases;

- Slanderous articles about me appearing in the press, which had a negative impact on my private life;

- Being subjected to numerous talks with KGB people at home, at work and at the police station, aiming to pressure me in the direction they found desirable;

- A burglary in August 1981 of my apartment in which valuables were stolen, but the Moscow district police department refused to confirm this fact at the inquiry of the State Insurance Office.

All these facts have predetermined my negative attitude towards the authorities and the KGB in particular, and that is why I refuse to answer any questions or cooperate in conversations. (That was not my sentence; the investigator had made it up himself, but I decided to leave it on the record.) I see this investigation as another link in the chain of the harassment that I described earlier.

Toward the end of the interrogation, I asked permission to go to the toilet, as I had heard that in this way you could find out if they were planning to arrest you (if they were, they would not let you go alone). I was allowed to go without an escort.

After the interrogation, Senior Investigator Yegorov, who was in charge of Repin's case, decided to talk with me. "I have come to get acquainted with you," he said. "I have heard that you try to avoid conflict with the authorities, but this time you seem to be carrying out some protest demonstration. Explain the reason for your behavior." I answered that he could find a detailed explanation in the protocol of the interrogation, but Yegorov insisted on talking with me, as a talk was preferable to a dry written account. I reiterated what was written in the protocol. Yegorov tried to convince me that the investigation had nothing to do with Israel and that I was to be investigated in connection with Repin's case anyway. After that, our talk went like this:

**Yegorov**: How many years have you been waiting for exit permits?

**I**: It has already been nine years and until now, I have not received a written answer from the OVIR (visas office).

**Yegorov**: Why do you need this scrap of paper? An oral answer is enough.

**I**: It is impossible to sue the OVIR in the absence of a written answer. Even a laundry will give you a receipt when you bring your wash to them.

**Yegorov**: You are breaking the law by refusing to give evidence.

**I**: Stop trying to make me cower in front of you.

**Yegorov**: You won't be allowed to leave for Israel until they finish investigating Repin's case.

**I**: I'm in no hurry now. My son was forcibly drafted into the Soviet army, and I am not going to go anywhere without him.

**Yegorov**: Everyone must serve in the Soviet army and your son is no different.

This was the end of my talk with Yegorov. "My" investigator escorted me to the room where I had been interrogated in order to sign the protocol. On the way there, we bumped into someone else who was being escorted to or from an interrogation. I was hurriedly ushered into a special recess so that we would not be able to see each other.

# 17.

# Burglary

In August 1981, our flat was burgled. We were not at home when the robbery occurred. The whole scene looked very strange, as if it had been staged: out of two pairs of jeans, one next to the other, only one was taken. There were two portable tape recorders, but, for unknown reasons, only one was stolen. Several other things were missing but nothing important; it was simply weird. We also noticed that the spy-hole in our neighbors' door was sealed from the outside with strips of paper. We reported the break-in to the police (Soviet militia, at that time). Two policemen came to take our testimony. Ida and I were taken to separate rooms, just as had occurred during the search.

To make a long story short, we remembered that our friend Ludmila Simovsky, also a refusenik, worked as an insurance agent. For a birthday present, she had presented me with an insurance policy for our apartment and all its contents. We contacted the insurance company, which said that they would need to request police confirmation of the theft before they could pay us compensation. However, the police refused to confirm the theft, their reason being that, "Aba Taratuta was an antisocial element and his life style proved him antisocial," whatever that meant. The insurance agent was very surprised and said it was the first time in her career that such a thing had happened.

This story was not over. Sometime later, we returned home and noticed that the spy-holes in the neighbors' doors were again plastered with paper. It seemed that a second attempt had been made to rob us, but, apparently, something prevented the thief or thieves from committing their crime.

However, the incident did not end there. A year and a half later, a police investigation led to a young man who was suspected of committing several robberies, including that of our apartment. They conducted an investigative experiment, during which the young man showed what he had taken and from where. Needless to say, we never received any compensation for our stolen property.

# 18.

# Our Contacts with the West

Help from the West for the Soviet Jews in their struggle for freedom of repatriation consisted of political, economic, and moral support. We believed that only publicity could protect us from the hostile totalitarian regime.

Our contacts with the West had begun immediately after we were refused permission to leave the Soviet Union in autumn, 1973, with a call from London. We found out much later that it had been Michael Sherbourne from the 35's Group (the Women's Campaign for Soviet Jewry) who had called. He spoke English (although he also knew Russian), and fear chalked Ida's face: she did not have adequate practice in communicating directly with English-speaking foreigners.

Then Tamara Brill and Jean Gaffin arrived from England. We have remained friends with these lovely women for many years. They visited us in Leningrad several times together with their husbands and children. In 1981, the Brill family moved to Israel, but kept in touch with us.

In December 1973, U.S. activist Shirley Goldstein with her daughter Gail visited us. Their tourist group stayed at the Leningrad Hotel, and Shirley invited us to drop by. In those days, to say the least, the authorities did not encourage Soviet citizens to come to Intourist hotels, where foreigners stayed. It was necessary to show one's passport at the entrance. That was the scariest part at that time—a strong form of psychological pressure. It meant that your cover was blown and you became "a person communicating with foreigners" and one never knew the consequences of that. That frightened many people.

During our visit to the hotel, Shirley presented us with a huge bag full of stuff that she had apparently collected from all her group; that made us feel very uncomfortable. We tried to refuse, but Shirley began to convince us that Jews had helped Jews from the beginning of time. "Tell me, Ida," she asked, "if not my, but your grandmother had emigrated from Russia, wouldn't you now be helping me?"

When we invited her to our home, we thought that our two-room flat where the three of us lived might look like a beggars' refuge in the eyes of a foreigner. We can safely say that we were mistaken. Subsequently, having been included in the lists of the various foreign Jewish organizations and a number of synagogues, we were invaded by their emissaries. During the visit of Irene Manekovsky, who headed the all-American organization, the Union of Councils for Soviet Jews, a memorable event occurred. Irene asked us to gather together our group of "refuseniks." After talking to us for a while, she sat down at the table and began to distribute checks, of twenty-five dollars per person.

The problem was that it was forbidden for Soviet citizens to have dollars or, in fact, any convertible currency at that time. However, bank checks could be exchanged for certificates that could be used in a special store called "Beryozka," where only foreigners could shop. There were plenty of imported goods, which could be bought by foreigners and those who had foreign currency given them by tourists.

At the beginning of the 1970s, there were organized parcels arriving in the Soviet Union through the "Dinerman" firm from London.[7] If a Jew requested an invitation from Israel, he also received a parcel by post, and it was possible to sell it for 200–300 rubles; that was good money at that time. However, some people used that "option" without any intention of leaving. I was asked to lead the fight against such "embezzlers." However, we refused to do this, because we realized that the loss to the charitable organizations behind these parcels was insignificant, but the propaganda effect would have been very negative.

The Soviet regime could not tolerate this long-term, organized support of Soviet Jews by foreign organizations; a black list was made and accordingly, parcels addressed to Jewish activists were soon confiscated. As we found our later, our family was also included on this list.

Representatives of the numerous western Jewish organizations usually came to the USSR as tourists. Foreigners brought valuable things like jeans, art albums, tape recorders, cameras, etc., as well as soup concentrates and white

---

[7]   This was the part of a combined program of the JDC and Israel of material help for Soviet Jews. The program was confidential and was called "Relief-in-Transit". (See M. Beizer, "Helping in Need and Struggle. The parcel program of the Joint Distribution Committee and 'Nativ' for Soviet Jews, in the 1950s to1970s," in *Jewish emigration from Russia, 1881–2005,* ed. O. Budnitsky (Russian) [Moscow, Rosspen, 2008], 220–240.—*Editor's note.*)

chocolate that could be put into parcels for sending to prisoners serving time for "illegal" activities. They brought Hebrew textbooks, Zionist literature, prayer books, and other religious objects. And they took away with them requests for invitations from Israel as well as letters of protest, appeals, and personal requests by refuseniks. We told foreign visitors about the latest events in our lives in the Soviet Union and discussed the best way the West could support our struggle.

The transfer of parcels brought in by foreign "emissaries" did not always proceed smoothly. Two young men from Norway arrived in Leningrad on a ship, while cruising on the Baltic Sea. They sent us a date to meet them at the seaport as they were transporting a hefty bag of Zionist literature. The fellows were told that passengers wishing to go ashore had to pass through customs control so they slung the backpack of banned books through the window onto the pier where we were standing.

The arrival in Leningrad in 1975 of a group of US activists consisting of the founders of regional committees for the defense of Soviet Jews made a big impression on us. This group included a scientist in the field of astronautics, Louis Rosenblum from Cleveland, a newspaper owner and editor, Si Frumkin from Los Angeles, who had a splendid knowledge of Russian culture, dentist Bob Wolf from Florida, and lawyer Zeev Yaroslavsky from San Francisco. Over the years, each one of them played a major role in the struggle for the right of Soviet Jews to emigrate.

In 1975, our friends Irina and Leonid Lotvin obtained permission to leave and immigrated to the United States. They made contact with Lynn Singer, the executive director of the Long Island branch of the Union of Councils for Soviet Jews. They established contact between Lynn and us, after which she called us regularly every two weeks for the next fifteen years and even came to Leningrad several times. We were so close to Lynn that she considered us as members of her family until her final days.

In our innocence, we thought that all Western public organizations that communicated with us (such as Union of Councils for Soviet Jews, National Conference for Soviet Jewry, Student Struggle for Soviet Jewry, "35's"—Women's Campaign for Soviet Jewry) closely co-operated with each other and shared the information that we transmitted by phone and with tourists. Unfortunately, as we found out later, the situation was completely different. Almost all of them competed with each other and fought for their spheres of influence. This applied in particular to the National Conference and less to everyone else. Fortunately, we did not know anything about this at the time.

Enid Wurtman and Connie Smukler visited us in 1976. Later in her memoirs, Enid wrote:

> "I loved having an opportunity to meet Aba and Ida! I remember Aba's *sefer* (book) for teaching Hebrew. I remember their warmth and good humor, their hopes to immigrate to Israel. I understood their trials and tribulations, all the impediments to their *aliya*; yet their determination to succeed and make *aliya* was firm. Aba and Ida inspired me with their heroism and their courage despite all the adversities and oppression they experienced. My heart went out to them and fueled my determination to return to the U.S. and fight for their freedom and immigration to Israel."

The stream of foreigners was such that in 1977 we created a "Guest book" in which we recorded the "who is who" and pasted business cards. This proved to be a good idea because it was impossible to remember all of them. During the fifteen years of our life as refuseniks, foreigners visited our house almost every week. Sometimes we even had three visits per day. In 1981, this guest book was confiscated during a search and we had to get a new book. Before our departure to Israel, we gave it to our guests Bunny and Frank Brodsky, and they safely took it out of the USSR. Had we taken the book with us, it would most certainly have been confiscated at customs control.

In 1980, the Israeli Esther Dorflinger came to us for the first time. I was not at home that summer as I was with a group of refuseniks in a village near Leningrad where we had contracted to build a wooden house. Esther told Ida that despite being a Jew, she accepted Jesus as the Messiah. She moved from the U.S. to Israel and traveled all over the world, preaching her beliefs and raising money for needy Jews. Esther visited us again when I was back home, and I asked her what exactly her mission was. When we clearly understood that she was not going to proselytize us, we became friends.

Esther visited us every year. Once she offered us 10,000 dollars. We refused to take it and explained to her that it was forbidden for USSR citizens to have a foreign currency. We suggested that she send the money to Lynn Singer. One day her friend, a very pleasant girl from Finland called Marike Romer who was from this missionary sect as well, showed up at our apartment without any advance notice. She gave us a box with paper napkins, which covered up ten-ruble banknotes—10,000 rubles (3,000 dollars) in total.

It was a very large sum of money for those times, when the average monthly salary in the country was 170 rubles, and a car cost 5,000 rubles. We were horrified, and explained to Marike that she could have been arrested at the border and begged her not to do it again. However, a year or two later, she repeated the same trick. Obviously, we distributed this money between everybody and it was spent on social needs.

Our friendship with Esther Dorflinger continued after we left the Soviet Union. We met various nationalities in her home, including Arabs. They professed one faith and loved Israel.

I remember the meeting, in the early 1980s, with U.S. Congressman Charles Vanik, who was one of the authors of the constitutional amendment connecting the right to emigrate from the USSR with granting the Soviet Union the status of a favored nation in world trade. The meeting took place in a hotel. The Congressman suggested that the United States should give the Soviet Union most favored nation status on condition that Jews received permission to emigrate. All of us objected to such an idea at first; let them grant Jews the right to emigrate and only after that, grant the Soviet Union most favored nation status. As we found out later, Charles Vanik talked about this to Jews in Moscow and Tbilisi, and their reactions were the same.

Sometime after Congressman Vanik's visit, a senator, Congressman Mark Levin, arrived on the same mission. I asked him whether he had read the book *The Twelve Chairs* by Ilf and Petrov, where the chairs are sold on the following conditions: money in the evening—chairs next morning. Obviously, my question caught him by surprise. When we were leaving after the meeting, the Congressman stopped me at the door and said that he will definitely read the book.

A visit of the well-known British historian and writer, the author of the seven-volume Winston Churchill biography (*Official Biography of Winston S. Churchill*), Sir Martin Gilbert, left a big impression on us. The first time he came to us was during a Hebrew lesson in 1983. After that, when coming to Leningrad (he came often, at least once a year), Martin always visited our home.

Prior to one of his last visits, he was warned not to visit Jewish refuseniks. It was the obvious way of putting pressure on a writer who has just started writing about the World War II period; Soviet leaders wanted him to praise Joseph Stalin's role in the victory over fascist Germany. They did not take into account, however, that Gilbert was not a person who would let himself be manipulated. Our meetings proceeded even after the prohibition—not in private houses, of course, but in different Leningrad cafes. Martin appeared to be quite a good conspirator, and it was always possible for us to escape "tails."

For many years, Martin Gilbert sent us either postcards, or short letters every week, no matter where he was in the world. Most remarkable was the fact that he decided to put numbers on each and every one of those cards, knowing well that all our correspondence was checked, especially foreign mail. Contacts with Martin proceeded even after our departure from the USSR. Ida and I developed a very special friendship with Martin which continued in Israel. Sir Martin Gilbert dedicated his sixth volume of his biography of Winston Churchill, *Finest Hour*, published in 1983, to Aba Taratuta and Yuli Kosharovsky *in friendship, and in hope.*

The visit of Marvin Verman from Philadelphia played a very important role. Almost all of our foreign visitors asked how they could help us. Apart from essential needs, such as books, Hebrew textbooks, prayer books, etc., questions connected with our struggle for departure were raised. When Marvin first visited us, we discussed the current situation in the Soviet Union for nine hours, sitting on a sofa in our apartment. We discovered that he had a perfect grasp of the nature of Soviet power and what strategy the West should adhere to in its opposition to the totalitarian regime. With Marvin on board, we were henceforth able to advise foreign visitors to turn at all times to the very person whose vision coincided with ours on all these questions. Our friendship with Marvin and his wife Leila continues as I write.

It was very noticeable that, in general, the Jewish community of Philadelphia was very active in helping Soviet Jews in their fight for the right to emigrate. In addition to Verman, Frank and Bunny Brodsky and others frequently visited us. One of their synagogues even adopted us.

Generally, we distributed things brought by tourists among the needy in the name of Lynn Singer, and we also sold some of them, sometimes through a secondhand shop. Donated money went into reproduction of textbooks of Hebrew and Jewish *samizdat*, payment of trips to visit prisoners of Zion, material aid for their families, and on parcels to prisons and labor camps.

Occasionally, we received helped from some Leningrad Jews who had succeeded in leaving the Soviet Union and brought donations to our common cause. For example, Alexander Geller left three hundred rubles before he left for the U.S., and Ernest Narymsky contributed his leaving parcel. Boris Ruchkan, who immigrated to the U.S., sent jeans with one of the tourists.

The American consulate in Leningrad maintained relations with Jewish activists. In the mid-1980s, the vice-consul was a Jew from San Francisco, Daniel (Dan) Grossmann. Dan Grossman was a charming young man who knew Hebrew and Russian. At the age of nineteen, he went to Israel for a year to study Hebrew. He also visited Russia, as a student, to improve his Russian. His Russian was so good that those who met him for the first time mistook him for a citizen of one of the Soviet Baltic republics.

His grandfather fled from Russia to China with his family after the revolution of 1917. His son, Danny's father, then moved to the U.S., where Dan was born. The family knew Russian, and Dan himself made great efforts to preserve it. Not only we but also our son Misha were friends with Dan. Misha, who was almost the same age as Dan, naturally shared common interests with him. Dan often invited us (and not only us) to his apartment and screened films that we could not see in the Soviet Union. He brought kosher wine for Passover and took part in the celebration. Sometimes he was invited to Jewish weddings.

The active participation of Dan Grossman in the Jewish life of refuseniks did not escape the attention of the Soviet authorities and, eventually, he was expelled from the Soviet Union. The occasion was the diplomatic scandal of 1986, when the Americans cut in half the Soviet Embassy staff, which comprised 110 people, many of whom worked, to put it mildly, in semi-legal diplomatic activity. Half of the staff of the Soviet Embassy in Washington, D.C., was thus expelled.

In response, the Soviet authorities decided to expel half of the staff of the American Embassy in Moscow. As there were only ten people, only five were involved: three from Moscow and two from Leningrad. One of those two was Dan Grossman.

A friend of ours, an artist, told us that he had heard that a diplomat of the American consulate was leaving Leningrad and that he was to be asked to take a baby doll to pass on to someone; inside this doll there would be something which would not be permitted by customs. We immediately called Dan on a payphone in the street and told him about it. As it turned out, the doll was not brought to him. Apparently, our conversation had been overheard. (A diplomat's phone, no doubt, was tapped). Later, we often met Dan in Israel and in the United States.

# 19.

# Three Demonstrations, 1987

In the mid-1980s, with the accession to power of Michael Gorbachev, the communist regime adopted a policy of "Perestroika and Glasnost" (Perestroika roughly means 'rebuilding, change of policy' and glasnost is something like openness). We decided that it was time to return to pressuring the government with demonstrations demanding free exit of Soviet Jews to Israel.

## *Demonstration, March 23, 1987*

The first demonstration was scheduled for March 23, 1987. A couple of days prior to the planned demonstration, the would-be participants got together at Lev Shapiro's apartment. They included Lilya, the lady of the house, Lena Keis–Kuna, Inna Rozhanskaya, Ida Taratuta, Michael Beizer, Boris Lokshin, and I. We decided to act in accordance with existing legislation. We sent the regional executive committee a request to allow us to spend an hour at the former Smolny Institute in order to protest against being forcibly detained in the USSR. Permission was not granted, but that could not stop us.

At 9:00 a.m., we lined up with posters of relevant content in front of the former Smolny Institute, which then housed the offices of communist party leaders in Leningrad and which essentially belonged to the city. Friends who had come to support us assembled at some distance. After a few minutes, a police squad arrived. A colonel of the militia, threatening us with arrest, demanded we disperse immediately. We refused. Then he threatened to take us to Smolny, to the head of the Department of Administrative Bodies of the Regional Committee of the Communist Party of the Soviet Union. To this we agreed, but said that we would come only in an hour, at the end of the demonstration.

The police retreated, giving way to a group of sturdy young men, surrounding us in a dense circle to hide us from the view of passers-by. They introduced themselves as tourists from Novgorod and diligently pretended that they were really interested in why we wanted to leave so great a country as the Soviet Union in order to go to Israel. We, in turn, pretended not to know who they were, and distributed Zionist propaganda among them. The hour thus passed in the skirmish with the "tourists."

The reception in the Smolny was the usual bureaucratic affair. The head of the Leningrad OVIR (visas office), Leonid Savitsky, declared that we had been refused exit visas in accordance with the law and that he did not see any reason to change their policy (in spite of this declaration, Michael Beizer received permission to leave a week later). We saw that the conversation was useless. I suggested that we leave the reception room, and we got up and left.

The next day, the radio station "Deutsche Welle" reported that there had been a free demonstration of Jews in the USSR, and that this reflects the democratic character of the new Soviet regime.

### *With slogans on the chest*

The newspaper *Vecherniy Leningrad* published a short piece called "With slogans on their chests" about our demonstration in which they described a group of people outside the Smolny Institute with slogans held against their chests reading "Let us go home" and "We demand reunification with family in Israel." The article continues in this vein.

This group was made up of so-called refuseniks; individuals who are currently not allowed to leave the Soviet Union. Do they encounter any obstacles? With this question our correspondent met with the head of OVIR, Leonid Savitsky who explained that there was no hint of any infringement of rights in this situation. He reminded our correspondent that the rules of travel of citizens of the Soviet Union were in strict accordance with the provisions of the International Covenant on civil and political rights, adopted by the UN General Assembly in December 1966 and these included certain restrictions on travel.

It was emphasized that each of the demonstrators had been repeatedly told by the local police why they had personally had their requests denied. These reasons appear, he continued, in the decree of the Council of Ministers of the USSR on amendments to the provision on the entry to and the departure from the Union of Soviet Socialist Republics. Departure is particularly not permitted if a citizen has knowledge of state secrets. An example of this is of a stoker in a bathhouse who is known still to have access to state secrets from his previous employment. Aba Yakovlevich Taratuta, a gas boiler operator who applied to be reunited with an aunt in Israel whom he had never even known, having been born ten years after her departure. From his previous work as a senior engineer in a scientific research institute he was still informed of various state secrets.

It is clear that these restrictions apply legitimately to several other members of the group in question and will do so for years to come. They know perfectly well that no violation of the law has occurred but they continue to rebel, aiming to draw attention to themselves by such actions.

The head of OVIR concluded the interview by saying that the USSR has recently taken, and will continue to take, further measures to simplify and reduce the duration and procedure of reviewing applications by citizens wishing to travel abroad.

He also gave our correspondent the following statistics: since January 1987, 167 Leningrad Jews have received permission to immigrate to Israel, despite which only two dozen of them have so far left the country.

## Demonstration, April 24 1987

Exactly a month later, on April 24, 1987, in the same place and under the same slogans, another demonstration took place. The difference consisted only in the fact that the number of participants had increased significantly; twenty-three Leningrad Jews came to the Smolny, unsuccessfully seeking the right to repatriation.

As previously, we tried to obtain permission from the city authorities and were refused. On the appointed day for the demonstration, I was suddenly called to the Executive Committee of our Moscow district. We decided to go there together and then go on to the Smolny.

I do not exactly recall the reason for the summons, but, after the visit, time was short. Boris Lokshin had arranged with the driver of a bus to take our group. On the way to Vosstaniya Square, the bus was stopped by police officers, ostensibly to check the documents of the driver. After another few hundred meters, the bus was stopped a second time. We decided not to wait and continued on foot.

We lined up, with placards in our hands. Suddenly there were cleaners with brooms who began to sweep the alley where we stood, sweeping away the dust and debris along with us. This garbage-disposal technique continued to force us from the area adjacent to the Smolny. Lokshin began to resent these actions loudly. Immediately, the police intervened, turned on him, and forced him into a car. A militiaman demanded that we split up. I asked him to let Lokshin go in exchange for the termination of the demonstration. He agreed.

## Demonstration, June 10, 1987

This demonstration was dedicated to the *azkara* (a remembrance ceremony thirty days after death) of a long-time refusenik Yuri Shpeizman. It was to be held at the Isaak square at the City Executive Committee building, with twenty-seven participants.

The Shpeizmans had been denied exit visas on the ground of secrecy: Yuri's brother had been working at the Kirov plant, which produced tanks and tractors. Some years before obtaining permission to leave the country, Yuri fell ill with an incurable blood disease and right before his departure he had a heart attack. Doctors had recommended against flying, but the desire to see their daughter, son-in-law, and grandchildren (whom they had never seen) in Israel was so great that the Shpeizmans decided to ignore the doctors' advice and on May 10, they flew to Vienna where Yuri tragically passed away, on the same day, in the airport.

Just after we lined up against the curb, a number of large water cannons for cleaning streets shot past us very close to the pavement. Two police buses into which we were promptly loaded followed them. Misha, who did not participate in the demonstration since he had already obtained an exit visa, asked to be detained together with the others. His request was granted.

They transported all of us to the local police station, compiled a police report with the charge of disturbing public order for each of us, and then let us go. A month later, everyone received a summons. The trial took several days and was carried out decently enough. Even the sentences were relatively mild— everyone was fined twenty-five rubles. During the court session, there was a funny episode. Chernoshvarts, when asked about party membership, answered that he was a member of the Gush Emunim Party.

Misha did not receive a summons to the trial but just two days before his departure for Israel, the telephone rang. A bossy male voice threatened to detain him at the airport if he was not tried and sentenced. There were serious doubts that they would let him leave after all.

The point was that, according to the Criminal Code of the RSFSR, the punishment in our case was "corrective labor." In the meantime, the validity of his exit visa would be in question. So Misha and I (without telling Ida) went to the district court, where we managed, despite the difficulties, to find his file and with even greater difficulties, to persuade one of the judges to conduct a "fair and speedy" trial—that is, to sentence my son to a twenty-five-ruble fine, which we immediately paid.

# 20.

# Not by Zionism alone

I cannot say we were totally occupied only by fighting the regime (which was continuing with variable success). We had quite a lot of friends, and we were still too young to abandon all the joys of life.

Our closest friends at the time were Ira and Leonid Lotvin, who lived not far from us in Leningrad. We often visited each other and spent much time together. We even applied for exit visas at the same time. After the Lotvins' departure to the U.S., Natasha and Eugene (Zhenya) Abeshaus became our closest friends. Zhenya's hobbies were mountain hiking and kayaking. He was also an avid cross-country skier. With the Abeshauses, we used to go kayaking, taking our kids with us. In 1976, they received exit visas and left for Israel. After their departure, we continued our kayaking with Anya and Roman Khaikin, and we, even went on two mountain tours in the Caucasus and the Carpathians.

In the summer of 1979, we invited two refuseniks, the mathematician Sergey Yuzvinsky and the linguist Igor Raikhlin, to go kayaking on the Zheymyane River in Estonia. Upon returning home, Sergey introduced me to his "club," a group of friends, who shared the same interest in downhill skiing and weekly visits to the Russian steam baths. The composition of this group was varied both socially and by ethnicity (Jewish and Russian), including refuseniks (Edward Markov, Ilya Simovsky, Sergey Yuzvinsky, etc.), and ordinary Soviet people (Boris Bovshevsky, Eugene Maksimov, and others).

For the winter skiing season, we rented a shed in the suburbs of Leningrad; it was actually a log hut with a wood-burning stove and wooden bunk beds, where eight people could sleep. In this cabin, we kept our skis and boots, which saved us the hassle of carrying them from the city. Nearby was a slope with a towrope ski lift, but it was for members only, so we generally clambered up on foot. The recognized leaders of our group were Volodya (Vladimir) Panchenko (nicknamed Syapa) and Sergey Yuzvinsky.

Volodya worked at a "secret" organization but was not afraid to be friends with Jewish refuseniks and was ready to help everyone. The only thing he would not do was visit my apartment, as this could have cost him his job. Sergey was a talented mathematician and a member of our scientific seminar for refuseniks. Under his guidance, I first tried downhill skiing (I had had experience with cross-country skiing from childhood).

In 1979, Yuzvinsky and his family received permission to leave the USSR, but he did not cancel our trips and went skiing. We were coming back by train when Sergey, who was usually very discreet in public, said that he was not worried about the fate of our group, as it could now rely on me. To hear this from a person who is usually very reserved was a great compliment.

Each year (and sometimes twice a year, in May and November) we went to Kirovsk or to one of the Caucasus Mountains ski resorts. At that time in the USSR, it was very difficult to get a voucher for a ski resort, and on arrival, to buy a ski lift pass. Sometimes we were lucky enough to borrow from professional athletes, and several times we even were able to get a room and ski passes in a downhill ski school in Kirovsk, where a good friend of ours worked as a coach.

It should be noted, that the quality of ski equipment in the Soviet Union was such that one could use it only at the risk of life and limb. Moreover, it was impossible to buy everything you needed at the store. If you were lucky enough to have some money, you could occasionally buy second-hand skis or boots from a good firm: this significantly reduced the risk of injury.

In the summer, we regularly went water skiing on a lake near Leningrad. We used a boat with two outboard motors owned by the organization where Ilya Simovsky worked. The boat and engines were about our age, so every trip to the lake began with repairs. One engine did not have enough power to pull the skier on the surface, but when the second motor became available (which did not always happen), the skier was able to glide on the surface of the water, holding the tether attached to the boat. First, we used two skis, but when the motion was fast enough we could throw off one ski and ski on the other one. It was an incredible sense of speed!

Once a week we visited the baths, where a group of refuseniks was working. We met on the day when the baths were closed to the public. At night, the steam room was stoked especially, for us, and we prepared brooms (bundles of birch tree twigs traditionally used in Russian steam baths) from the summer greenery. Ilya Simovsky explained to us that one did not go to wash but to steam and to drink tea or beer. These sessions lasted four hours. Sometimes we celebrated birthdays there.

Typically, at each of the three events—the baths, downhill skiing, and water skiing—there was a different group of participants. But the core of five or six "founding fathers" remained unchanged. I became good friends with all of them very quickly. After the departure of Sergey Yuzvinsky, I invited some of my friends, who successfully blended into our company.

Our other close friends, Fanya and Mark Berman, lived in the city of, Petrozavodsk in the Republic of Karelia. They had both graduated from the Leningrad Medical Institute and, as Jews, they knew they would be unable to receive work assignments in Leningrad. They were sent to Petrozavodsk, and eventually a close group of young Jewish people evolved around them. The Bermans decided not to return to Leningrad and stayed in Petrozavodsk, working there as doctors until 1995, when they immigrated to Israel.

Mark was an extraordinary person. He was fond of ski touring and made amateur movies of Karelia, which won prizes at the All-Union competitions. We used to visit them often, and once we went together on a kayak trip on Lake Onega around the famous island of Kizhi, which is a museum of very beautiful wooden churches built in the eighteenth and nineteenth centuries. It was amazing that in almost every village, Mark knew somebody and had many friends among the locals.

Most of these people were very nice, close to us in spirit, and although in time, life dispersed us to different countries, we have maintained and cherished our friendships. Many people visited us in Israel: from the U.S.—Natasha and Boris Likhtik, Ludmila and Ilya Simovsky, Anna and Anatoly Molot, Eugene and Abram Kagan, Frieda and Mark Budnyatsky, Alya and Sergey Yuzvinsky, and Natan Rodzin. From Russia came Slava Kogan and Alexander Geller and from Germany—Leonid Sorokopud.

## Shabashka

*Shabashka* is a moonlighting job carried out by a group of people who work together, usually at building something, away from big cities. People did this when on leave or students during their vacations.

## *Memories of Nathan Rodzin*

Former Leningrad refusenik with a decade of experience (refused immigration for ten years); since 1988 he has lived in the U.S.

When we became "refuseniks," it was clear from the start that it would be a long process. We had to find jobs that would take up little time, allow us to tend to our own affairs and make a little money on the side, as we realized that those would be poorly paid jobs. We therefore decided to try building houses in the countryside. We saw it as a sure way of making good money, for it was known that people who knew how to build houses, and knew other useful trades, could earn a fair amount. That was what we thought.

Because I knew that both Andrei Leshchinsky and Arik Shifrin had once worked on construction sites in the *virgin lands* (vast, untilled lands of Kazakhstan and parts of Siberia where students were sent in the summer to do construction and agricultural work) and, as Andrei claimed to have been a great specialist in the building of wooden houses, we decided that that was the thing to do. They both claimed that the work was good and that the cut wood smelled nice.

I thus called for others to join us. I remember that some people came to me to enroll but, frankly speaking, none of us had ever tried building houses, except maybe as a onetime summer job while in college. Aba Taratuta, Arik Shifman, Andrey Leshchinsky, and I were there initially. Then Edward Markov and Stas Yarzhembovsky joined us. More people came later: even Misha Taratuta worked there for some time. Yevgeny Lein came later, as far as I remember. The rest joined only part time. Leonid Sorokopud would come at weekends, and it seems to me, Ilya Simovsky came once.

We all assembled there, got our names on the list, and then started to look for a *khaltura*, a side job of the kind we had in mind, although I do not remember how we found it. Someone in the bunch was from the village Siverskaya, and, I think, Andrey Leshchinsky went with him, saw the site, and arranged things with the foreman.

There was another problem. The army was after Arik and Andrey. There was the so-called "Khrushchev draft," in which university and college graduates were drafted as lieutenants. They were already chasing them, sending them draft notices. They quit their jobs, took their employment records with them and handed them over to the local authorities of the village Siverskaya. The advantage of work in the countryside is that they do not inform the central police whom they employ, even though they are supposed to do so within three days. I also started getting worried. The local authorities were getting curious about me; they sent their people to find out whether I was "a parasite."

I clearly remember our first day on the job. We, a bunch of Jews, with only Stas and Andriusha (Andrei), at the head, came to the place where there was a team of carpenters repairing the next-door building. They were completely stunned when they saw us. Andriusha, who had Slavic looks and knew the ways of the common Russians—he had spent considerable time at building jobs in villages—came up to them, lifted a huge log that four Jews were unable to lift later, made a round with it, dropped it and spat with great gusto. He was greatly respected after that. They called him Andreich and asked him for advice. Physical strength is greatly valued in Russia.

I think our team's arrival and our daily "attempts" at constructing a house radically changed the local team's everyday life. It got more exiting: they never stopped watching us and wondering. They were always especially astonished at the sight of four Jews moving a heavy log from point A to point B: in order to do that, they first gathered round the log, discussed the problem for about ten minutes, then approached the log from different angles, trying to find the best position to pick it up, changed sides, put the log on four different shoulders and finally moved it to point B, after which each side tried to throw it down in the opposite direction, which was impossible, because the log lay on different shoulders. It must have been quite a sight!

In short, we never failed to astonish the local team. They were so shocked that they even stopped drinking for a while. We were known as "the Armenian team" because they were unable to imagine that Jews could build anything: "Jews could only fuck you over."

Very soon, both the Siverskaya village residents and the office that had employed us realized that the men who had come to build the house were not descendants of Kizhi builders. Their genetic stock just did not contain any carpenter genes.

We were supposed to build a new two-story, fourteen-apartment building, while they were refurbishing an old building that stood close to the one we were working on.

I remember that the local team was constructing scaffolds, without handrails and walking on them without falling. In America and India, they build scaffolds without rails, and people do not fall off; they can even walk along a pole. But this does not matter.

The process was organized like this: we did not have to peel the bark off the logs, for they brought us beams hewn on two sides. These were poor-quality beams, made of equally poor timber. The bosses sold all the good stuff on the black market or kept it for their own use, providing our project only with low quality materials.

First, we dug two deep holes for the toilets, and then we built the framework for the foundation. They brought us the concrete and we pushed it in wheelbarrows and poured it into the framework.

Then we started to put up the beams. It all went well at first; the walls did not look curved, but later, when we had to erect them higher, we found out that we were lacking the necessary skills and physical strength. They therefore provided us with a simple crane called "Pioneer"; installing it also required some effort. We had to build a tower for that crane. I climbed the tower to fix the crane on it. I have a photo of this. We used a pulley to lift the crane. We shouted: *vira, maina*, like dockers. (The phrase *maina, vira* means "to water, to the air" in Aramaic and it came to Russia from Italian dockers, who had adopted it from Phoenician sailors.) Only we did not know which was "up!" and which was "down!" so making rules took time. If you were off guard when lifting the load and did not stop the crane on time, the crane's arm would swing to the other side.

There were some problems with the equipment. For example, we had a gasoline powered saw that had to be "re-kindled" from time to time, and this was Andriusha's job: he blew through the spark plugs, overheated it and burned something. We also had an electric saw but it was a weak one. It was huge and would stall immediately and it was not sharpened in the bargain. However, we were gradually moving on, even though the saw's chains broke down frequently. We found a man in the village who fixed those chains. It did not cost us a penny because he worked for the same office.

How was our everyday life organized?

I had a wagon and there was somebody else with me. I remember: it was Andrei. I clearly remember how he recited Goethe by heart. Others slept in a house, and we played bridge on its veranda. Andriusha and I slept in the wagon, as did one of the weekend workers.

One of our weekend guests was "caught red-handed" by Ivan, the local team's second foreman, when he came to our wagon to sharpen the axe, because the grindstone was in our wagon. Everyone was already out working, and a friend of ours was standing there with his pants down and putting baby cream on his rear end. After that, Ivan went out and said,

"Sure, they are all Armenians—ass fuckers."

We soon realized that we would not earn a lot of money. Sometimes we received an advance. It somewhat rekindled our enthusiasm, which was dying quickly. The woman who came to the site to check matters did not talk to us; she spoke only with Andriusha:

"Andrei Nikolayevich, why is there a curvature in the wall?"

Andriusha answered, unmoved:

"No one is going shoot from it, are they?"

This folk wisdom convinced her, and she left us in peace for a while.

When we got to the second story, it got really tough, I remember.

Our everyday life, however, was going along nicely. At the start, our lunch was a crazy thing because we cooked according to Andriusha's system: everyone threw into a pot with boiling water whatever he thought appropriate. The result was terrible. Even now, I cannot even think of Bulgarian canned baked beans in tomato sauce, which I hated.

Then we arranged with the nearby kindergarten that they would give us cereals for breakfast and we would saw and chop firewood for them in return.

In short, the work went slowly, unreasonably slowly, considering how many we were on the job. I remember that Aba did the scribing, and as he knew math, the logs sometimes did fit well at the joints, but sometimes they fell apart because of the faulty measuring tools.

We made the joint in the beam's middle, the dovetail being the lock. It is a rather complicated geometric pattern that can be made with a precise axe blow at a certain angle, so Andriusha made a gauge with which we marked the beams, but he often said, when he saw the result, that we had better cut that dovetail off and take a new log.

We used to go to the river. The sanitary conditions were terrible, I remember. Andriusha shared with us his experience of working under rough conditions. One of his recommendations was to use one end of the towel for the feet, the other for the face, and change sides after a week, and that is what we did, quite successfully.

People came at weekends: Vitold Brushtunov, his wife Ira Levitina, who was an international chess grandmaster, her sister Lena, and someone else. We were preparing for a bridge (a popular card game) championship.

Then there was a conflict with the local team. Andrei and I left for the bridge championships in Leningrad and decided to stop work for that time because without Andrei nobody knew what to do. When we came back, we found out that our timber was missing. Kolya the foreman was on holiday and Ivan his assistant succumbed to greed and sold our beams to the owner of the next-door house.

I remember this brawny man who used to do his daily dozen on his porch every morning. That was the man to whom our logs went.

We went to sort out things. Yevgeny said, "Ivan, aren't you ashamed of yourself?" And so it went on. As it did not help, in order to avoid these problems in the future, we had to give him a smack on the face, as Academician Pavlov had advised. This did not help, either, so for half a day we just sat and smoked. That was the work conflict we had.

We started the work sometime in the beginning of the summer, perhaps in June. I remember that the weather got bad, it was raining, and the fellows' enthusiasm slackened very soon. It was cold. The autumn came. We had not even started the roof or the heating stove. I do not remember what height we got up to with the construction, but we certainly did not finish the house; someone else had to do it.

Then they delayed our pay, a big sum.

I do not remember how much I earned, but it was striking that in the end we did earn some money—you see, it was the first time we had ever held axes. After some time, I stopped going there. Andrei Leshchinsky was among the steadiest; he stayed. We decided afterwards that he deserved better pay because he took the trouble to instruct and teach us. By the end, only Yevgeny Lein stayed there with him. Andriusha said: "Everyone dropped out, only Lein continued to come—an iron man." Even now, he remembers it. I met him when I visited Leningrad in 1996.

## *A Journey to the Six Republics*

In the summer of 1982, while our son Misha was serving in the army, we decided, together with Boris Likhtik, that we would travel to six republics of what is today the former USSR. Our departure had been delayed for a long time, as we naively hoped that Misha would receive the short leave promised him by the military. Our hopes were in vain, and finally, we hit the road without him.

The purpose of our trip was to establish personal contacts with fellow refuseniks, prisoners of Zion, or with their families. We wanted to support them morally, to ascertain their needs, and then try to help them. Each republic had its own specific characteristics. The Jewish emigration activists in major cities of the western areas of the Soviet Union, particularly in Moscow and Leningrad, were better protected than elsewhere, because connections had been established with foreign correspondents from the U.S. and Europe. In addition, the mainstream of envoys from international Jewish organizations flowed to this part of the country. Therefore, the activists from the periphery felt abandoned and were in need of support.

We started with Tallinn, capital of Estonia, where we had friends, Sima and Boris Yudeikin. They themselves were not refuseniks, but some mutual friends, refuseniks from Riga, had introduced us to the Yudeikins. In those years, Tallinn, as the entire Baltic region, appeared to us as a part of the Western World. We met with a group of young people who wanted to immigrate to Israel. They had many questions for us and we tried to give them all the available information. A big surprise to us was that there was a private, non-commercial sauna there. It was built in the basement of their apartment house, and each apartment could use it on demand. Naturally, we asked to use it during our visit.

Our next stop was in Riga, where for a long time we had had many friends. On the way to Riga, we stopped at a roadside restaurant with a shop. This shopping complex belonged to one of the Latvian collective (or maybe state) farms, and they sold some farm produce that was unfamiliar to us, such as smoked chicken and homemade beer.

In Riga, we stayed with Judith and Haim Solovey. They had just celebrated the bat mitzvah of their eldest daughter Dana. Haim, hearing our praises of the smoked chicken, gave us a smoking grill of his own making, which could be used at home on a gas stove. We met many friends of ours: Fanny and

Alexander Maryasin and their daughter Faina, Jamie and Fima Goldberg, Senya Shvartsband, Israel Deyft, Ira Lebedeva, and her daughter Olga. When Olga's husband, Lev Fabrikant, heard that we were going to Lvov, he promised to connect us with his brother.

We then stopped at Vilnius. Not sure that our friends would provide us with shelter; we found a vacancy at a suburban hotel and thus solved the problem of lodging. In the city, we met with Alla Fel, who organized an *ulpan* for Hebrew instruction. We decided to visit Carmela and Vladimir Raiz. We had been warned that they led a secluded life and it would not be easy to meet with them. When we came to them without an invitation, they did not open the door to us, but later they received us very warmly. We discussed our common problems and agreed to maintain contact.

We next went to Lvov. The brother of Lev Fabrikant helped us find a good hotel and came to visit us. He told us about the situation in the city and the intensive influx of tourists from neighboring countries. He himself was a successful playwright; his plays appeared constantly on the stages of theaters in Lvov, and elsewhere. At the beginning of his theatrical career, when preparations were underway for staging one of his plays, he was summoned to the Department of Culture in Moscow. There he was told that the name of Fabrikant is not suitable for a Soviet playwright and was asked to pick another one that would sound more Russian. He mulled over in his mind some of the most popular anecdotal Russian names—Ivanov, Petrov, Sidorov.... As the first two names had already been taken by Jewish playwrights, he had to choose the name Sidorov. Under this name, he continues to appear on posters. For him, repatriation to Israel was not even a consideration.

Our route then took us to Bendery, where Ida Nudel had taken refuge after her release from exile in Siberia. She was forbidden to live in big cities, including in her former Moscow residence. During her exile, and here in Bendery, her friends from Moscow and Leningrad frequently visited her, helping as much as they could to alleviate her plight.

On the way there, we stopped in the city of Chernovtsy to have a look at the old synagogue, which was later rebuilt as a theater. We were allowed inside and saw what had been done to this beautiful building. The synagogue had two floors, but now neither the second floor nor the balcony existed. It turned out that they had simply eliminated the overlap between the first and second floors. By doing this they, of course, ruined the acoustics, but it seems that no one really cared.

Ida Nudel was very glad to see us. She introduced us to some local refuseniks, Riana and Slava Royak and Anna and Michael Liberman, whom Ida, with her fighting character had rallied around herself in the struggle to immigrate to Israel. They indignantly told us about the Soviet Nazi rally in Bendery and were very concerned about this.

Our next stop was in Kishinev, where the family of a Prisoner of Zion housed us, Vladimir Zukerman. It turned out that they were in dire need of some medicine that it was impossible to acquire locally, so upon our return to Leningrad, we bought and sent them the drugs.

Next, we visited Lisa Shnirman, whose husband Simon was convicted for refusing to serve in the army and had served time in a prison camp instead. Lisa lived in a tiny room with a small child under horrible conditions. We promised to help her by conveying information to the West about her conditions. There were more meetings with other refuseniks in Kishinev, after which we went on to the city of Minsk.

As Minsk was more than a day's drive away, we had planned to spend the night in the woods in a tent, which we had with us. However, it started to rain so heavily that the three of us had to sleep in the car. Surprisingly, this was possible. We got up early and drove on. Rain continued to drizzle, and we drove somewhat above the speed limit. After a while, when driving past a police station, our car and the car ahead of us were stopped. The two people from the other car, and Boris and I, were summoned to the station. First, the young lieutenant gave a speeding ticket to the drivers of the other car and sent them away. Then it was our turn.

Boris at the time had been working as an ambulance driver, and a speeding ticket could eventually cost him the loss of his professional driver's license. Therefore, we said that I was behind the wheel. The lieutenant began to draw up a report and, having learned my name, asked about its origin. He thought I was at Tatar. When he found out that I was Jewish, he said that there are rumors that Jews, like the Tatars, eat dogs. I therefore had to deliver a lecture to him on *kashrut* (Jewish Dietary Laws), which he listened to with great interest. Then something unexpected happened: the lieutenant said that we were good people, he liked us, and he tore up the report. He then warned us that we should comply with traffic rules because the road is slippery and this morning in his area, there had already been two serious accidents.

Unexpectedly, the knowledge of the laws of kashrut thus helped us avoid trouble. After this, there was another similar incident, which ended the same way. At this point, Boris really believed in the good luck that had accompanied me throughout my whole life.

In Minsk, as in all previous places, we learned the needs of local activists: Bielsky brothers, chess master Boris, and others. We visited the old synagogue, which was in a neglected condition, and a monument to the Jews killed during the German occupation ("The Pit").

From there, we went to Alushta in the Crimea. Here we had a rest after our long trip and celebrated the Jewish New Year on the beach, with the traditional honey and apples. From Alushta we went to Sevastopol, where Boris's wife Natasha and his daughter Katya were waiting for us in the resort village of Uchkuevka. We stayed there at a campsite where we met our refusenik friends from Leningrad: Frieda and Mark Budnyatsky, and Natasha and Michael Strugach.

## *An Expedition to Siberia*

Before leaving for the U.S., Sergey Yuzvinsky managed to join a geological expedition to Siberia, and he gave me the phone numbers of geologists who worked at the Russian Geological Research Institute (VSEGEI) with whom he went on the expedition. In 1985, after realizing that I was not going to be sent to Siberia in chains, I decided to follow Sergey's footsteps and went on a similar expedition as a cook and part-time worker together with a friend of mine, a student by the name of Misha Krivonosov. In addition to us, the party consisted of three geologists: two women (a PhD and a post-graduate student) and a young man.

We flew to the Siberian city of Irkutsk, and settled on the base of the Institute a few miles from the city. We were supposed to reach a certain village on the Lena River, but in that year, there had been a big fire in the *taiga*, and travel was impossible. We spent two weeks on the base, and during that time managed to make a trip to Lake Baikal, about which legend has it that it is impossible to swim there because the water is always too cold. The rumors were greatly exaggerated—we did manage to swim in the lake, perhaps because the summer was so very hot.

When the fire slackened, we arrived at the train station of Ust-Kut; from there we sailed by boat down the Lena River. Smoke still drifted above the surface of the river, but we managed to get to our destination. Our geologists were involved in the description of rock samples collected in the local repository; Misha and I were to serve them meals. The situation in our party was very unpleasant because our geologists happened to be very antisemitic. With me, they behaved correctly, but poor Misha suffered from them greatly.

## A Black Sea Cruise

On August 3, 1987, we said goodbye to our son Misha, who left for Israel. We were not in the best of spirits, as we did not know when we would be able to see our son again. To unwind a little, we decided to take a short vacation at the Black Sea, thanks to the flexible schedule at my place of work. There, by a very happy coincidence, we bought discount vouchers for a one-week cruise from Odessa to Batumi.

In Odessa, we visited some of our refusenik friends (David Shechter and others) and boarded the cruise ship called the "Nadezhda Krupskaya" (named after the widow of Vladimir Lenin). The ship was very old and was not certified for use as a cruiser, but for tourists from the so-called "People's Democracies," the Soviet Union permitted the violation of international norms. The ship had been chartered for a tourist group from Romania, but at the last moment, the Romanians canceled their order, fearing a cholera epidemic in Odessa.

The ship sailed at night and by day cast anchor at the next port. This cruise made an indelible impression on us. The restaurant handed out menus, and you could order dishes for the next day. The ship had a swimming pool and a casino, to which the Soviet people, "builders of communism," flocked. But what surprised us most of all is that you could order coffee at the buffet, drink it, and leave the empty cup anywhere you pleased, and nobody would say a word. There was a feeling that we had briefly entered another world.

From Batumi, we went back to Novy Aphon (New Athos), where we met with refusenik friends, Samoilovich from Moscow and Lilya Shapiro from Leningrad. A few days later, Lilya told us that she had phoned her mother in

Leningrad, who had told her that OVIR was looking for us. Apparently, they had finally given us permission to leave the USSR. We thought it over and decided that, as we had been waiting for them for fifteen years, we would let them wait for us for a few days.

Upon our return to Leningrad, we indeed received a call from OVIR, and they told us to reapply for an exit visa, because, as they said, our application had become outdated. After some arguing, we decided not to insist and asked Misha to send us a new invitation, which he did.

We had no problems arranging our departure. At the Pulkovo airport, the customs official took out and meticulously checked all the contents of our luggage and handbags. After finishing her inspection, she sat at a table at the far corner of the room and ordered us to repack our things. Then I placed my Leningrad notebooks in one of the suitcases. On January 3, 1988, we landed in Vienna, where the Israeli consul met us. We had a few hours before our flight and we managed to speak with him.

# 21.

# Israel

After Misha had been given permission to leave the USSR, we received a phone call from Enid Wurtman, a Soviet Jewry activist. Born in Brooklyn, she had repatriated to Israel with her husband Stuart and her children, where she worked with the Public Council for Soviet Jewry and continued to maintain contact with refuseniks in the USSR. Enid asked Misha in which absorption center he would like to live. Misha chose Tel Aviv. When we got to Israel, Enid asked us the same question. Naturally, we also preferred Tel Aviv.

Soon after our arrival, at Lynn Singer's initiative, Yuri Shtern, Yosef Mendelevich, and Shmuel Azarkh offered me the post of "Minister of Foreign Affairs" at the Information Center, a public organization that was founded and supported by Lynn Singer. I refused, explaining that this kind of work did not suit my nature. The same people later organized the "Zionist Forum" with Anatoly (Natan) Sharansky heading it. Eleven individuals, including myself, were elected to the Forum's presidium. They started holding regular meetings in Jerusalem, but I failed to report to the first one and they stopped inviting me.

After that, my cousin Tolya Epstein tried to recruit me to the Tehiya party, with the same outcome. As a result, I was completely freed from any public activity.

We started our life in Israel in Beit Brodetsky, a prestigious absorption center in North Tel Aviv, where we attended Hebrew classes. Hardly had we entered into the learning routine when Lynn Singer and Rita Eker from London invited us to visit Britain and the U.S. During this visit, we participated in the campaign for liberating Soviet Jews who were still denied the right to repatriate, and we were also able to express our gratitude to overseas activists for the help they had given us.

Upon our return, I started looking for a job. I was ready to accept the first offer, and I was looking forward to becoming a bathhouse boiling room operator. As fortune would have it, my CVs, which had been sent out before our *aliya*, had reached the Haifa Technion and Bezek, the Israeli telephone company. After an interview at the Technion and a written test at Bezek, both were ready to employ me. I chose the Technion: my knowledge of the programming language FORTRAN suited them.

Alas, little did I know then what salaries and pensions Bezek paid to their employees! I worked for the Technion for twelve years, even though my first boss explained to me from the start that nobody really needed me there. And he was right. They fired me four times, every time miraculously restoring me to my job.

When I went to Russia with an Israeli delegation in 1992, my friends who were still living there invited me to "our" Leningrad bathhouse, which had been privatized by then. Every year I go skiing in Europe with Edward Markov, who lives in Haifa as Ida and I do. Slava Kogan also joined us once. In addition to Edward Markov, some other old friends live in Israel now, among them Galya and Alec Zelichonok and Nora and Sergey Rotfeld. Starting from 1993, as I was employed only part time at the Technion, I looked for additional employment. In 1994, my friend Benjamin Kantor and I started a project in one of the technological "hothouses," where, within three years, we designed a device for underwater communication between frogmen.

In 1997, I started teaching math at a junior high school (grades 7–9) belonging to the "Mofet" school network that specialized in teaching physics and mathematics. The classes were supposed to be in Hebrew. This, however, was not the greatest problem in my career as a math teacher. The real problem was the discipline; I could not convince the students to keep quiet. These charming youngsters took my measure at once. No, they never jeered at me but their classroom behavior was, to put it mildly, uninhibited. No matter how much I racked my brains to get them interested and keep them quiet, it was all useless. This was a health-destroying job; a day of teaching cost me a kilo and a half of body weight. But being a masochist, I got used to this work and even came to like it.

In 2000, I retired from the Technion, but I continued to teach math and quit the school in 2001, after the accident with our son Misha.

Misha found a good job in the U.S.: he was the art director of the magazine *Playbill* and everything was wonderful, but in July 2000, Aba and Ida visited him in the States. On the second day, Misha and I went out to buy something in a store. We crossed their street, and an iron fence from the roof of a five-story house fell on Misha's head and then on Aba's neck. We both stayed alive, but Misha was in a coma for a month. He underwent fifteen operations and his left side was paralyzed. It is a miracle he can still function in spite of all the problems he still has.

Later Misha wrote a book in comic form about his experience in the hospitals, which is available on Amazon.*

Ida did not succeed in finding a job in her specialty and found employment at a local library. The workday there lasted four hours, but the pay was accordingly low. When we came to Israel, Ida was fifty-eight years old. In Israel, you have to work for ten years minimum in order to obtain a state pension. After seven years of work at the library, Ida reached the retirement age and was fired, three years before she was entitled to a pension. She subsequently taught English to young children for some time, but she was still not entitled to a pension.

One day one of our acquaintances, Inna Rozhanskaya-Lobovikov, came to visit us and told us that on the way to our place, she saw an album with photographs lying near an overfull garbage can, and the pictures were being blown by the wind across the street. It looked to her as if an old man or woman had died, and the album was being thrown away by the family as unnecessary. "The same will happen to us," she said. "We shall die, and our children will throw away our papers and old photographs; there won't be any traces left of us and of what we've been through." We started discussing this subject, and she suggested setting up an archive of materials on the Soviet Jews' struggle for their right to leave for Israel while those who participated in the events of the 1960s–80s were still alive.

At first Ida and I thought: who will want it? There are archives of the Israeli Liaison Bureau (known in Hebrew as *Nativ*), which had had been dealing with this topic for dozens of years. There are also the "Central Zionist Archive" and the archives in the universities….Why create something else?

We decided to consult our friend Dr. Michael Beizer, who was a historian. He said that not everything had been collected and certain materials were still

---

\* https://www.amazon.com/Practically-Bulletproof-Michael-Taratuta-ebook/dp/B004A1569U/ref=sr_1_6?ie=UTF8&qid=1476690521&sr=8-6&keywords=taratuta
*Practically Bulletproof* by Michael Taratuta. Highly recommended; editor.

unavailable. Although it meant a lot of difficult work, he would be ready to help us if we undertook it. Having secured consent from additional friends, Ludmila and Edward Markov, Mara and Pasha Abramovich, Inna and Igor Uspensky, and Alec Zelichonok, we started collecting material on the subject, which at first we kept in our apartment.

On April 22, 2002, we registered an association called *"Remember and Save,"* so that our project would gain official recognition. In the association's statute, we stated that its goal was the collecting and preserving of documents that reflected the struggle of Soviet Jews for their right to repatriate and for full Jewish life in the USSR. These documents would include lists of refuseniks and Prisoners of Zion, petitions, letters of protest and appeals to the Soviet authorities, Jewish organizations and public bodies in the West and in Israel, photographs, audio- and video-recordings, the Jewish *samizdat,* memoirs, diaries, interviews with the movement's participants, and materials documenting the international support for the Jewish movement in the USSR.

A working group comprising fifteen individuals was established. Besides the aforementioned friends, it included Natasha and Eugene Abeshaus and Roman Levin, who was in charge of the video recordings database. Tamara Brill and Donna Wosk edited English texts, while Lena Romanovsky did a fine job of translating Russian texts into English. Anatoly Shidlovich typed Russian interviews. We were getting a good deal of help as well from Sergey Komov, who helped us with computer work.

Since the founding of the Association, we have managed to collect thousands of documents, photographs, memoirs, and other materials from over three hundred private collections of the former participants of the Jewish movement in the USSR. Ida and I recorded about a hundred interviews with former activists residing in Israel and the U.S. A computer database in three languages—Russian, English, and Hebrew—has been created. Our archive materials can be found at the Association's website,* managed by Edward Markov as editor and webmaster. Vladimir Kremer, a member of the association, prepares material for the Israeli Russian-language newspaper *Vesti* and an Internet site.

---

* www.soviet-jews-exodus.com

Most activists of American, British, and French Jewish organizations who supported us in the years of "refusal" agreed to become honorary members of the board of directors. There was only one who refused—David Bartov, the former head of the Israeli "Liaison Bureau." He did not believe that our undertaking would yield any fruit.

At first, our expenses were modest—telephone, post office, trips. We received substantial financial help from Shirley Goldstein (Omaha, Nebraska, U.S.) and Enid Wurtman mobilized support for us from Jerusalem. Thanks to their support, we were able to rent an office in Haifa and buy a computer and a digital camera. We never asked for money, but some people sent it nevertheless, although such cases were rare.

In 2007, at our initiative and with our active participation, a large exhibition called "The Jews of Struggle" was displayed at the Diaspora Museum in Tel Aviv. The exhibition was devoted to the forty-year anniversary of the revival of the Jewish national movement in the Soviet Union. Natan (Anatoly) Sharansky headed the preparation committee. Over one thousand people attended the opening of the exhibition, including former activists from the USA, Canada and Britain. The exhibition lasted seven months and was visited by Israeli schoolchildren, students and soldiers. An international academic conference devoted to the same subject was held in the framework of the exhibition. An excellent catalog of the exhibition was published in Hebrew, English, and Russian.

# Afterword

Years have passed. Many episodes from our life in the USSR have already been erased from our memory. We have long become accustomed to living here in Israel. When we lived in the Soviet Union, we did not call it "our land." For us, it was not our mother but more like a stepmother. To be part of a minority is the same as living in exile. We lived there in internal exile. When Russian antisemites shouted at us, "Scram to your Israel!" they were giving us the right advice. They lived in their country and it was useless to argue.

In Israel, we feel at home. Finally, we can walk with head held high. There is no longer the sense of a hostile environment. Now we feel as equal citizens of this, our country.

In all these years, I visited Russia only once, in 1992, I was a member of special delegation from Israel. Ida never and under no circumstances would agree to accompany me. I understood her.

For me it is difficult to understand people who go there willingly. It is like nostalgia for the prison in which you spent part of your life. It is probably nostalgia for youth. Here it feels so good to be a part of the majority—of our own majority.

*Haifa, 2012*

# Aba's refusenik diary

### August 1972

Authorities introduced taxes on education. My wife Ida and I resigned from our jobs at our secret (classified work) enterprises. We asked for an invitation from Israel. I went to take courses for (professional) drivers Class III, and Ida got a job at a post office.

### May 1973

We submitted papers for exit visas to leave for Israel for my mother Fanya, our twelve-year old son Misha, and the two of us.

### August 1973

The head of the visas office (OVIR in Russian), V. Bokov, verbally informed us that we could not leave the USSR because of our security clearances. We complained to the Regional Communist Party Committee (*Obkom* in Russian).

### February 1974

The chief of the *Obkom* public relations department informed us that we would never obtain anything in writing from them.

### February 1974

Without any warning, our telephone was disconnected for two years. The district office informed us that there was no technical possibility for reconnecting our line.

### December 1974

The district police station restricted us from leaving town because of an upcoming visit to Russia of U.S. president Richard Nixon.

## Spring 1975

New restrictions on leaving Leningrad were put into effect due to an upcoming culture symposium organized by refuseniks in Moscow.

## December 1975

A call came from OVIR for a two-hour chat with the deputy chief, Vorotyntsev. He tried to persuade us to resubmit documents and to be in touch with our former employers.

## January 1976

We sent an appeal to the Commission for the review of workers' rights on the eve of the Communist Party Congress.

## January 1976

We received a formal repudiation of our appeal to the commission by OVIR.

## March 1976

We made an appeal to our former employers.

## April 1976

Our telephone was disconnected for the second time, again without warning, for two years.

## May 1976

My wife received a reply from her former place of employment.

## December 1976

My wife and I were summoned to the Leningrad City Prosecutor's office for interrogation as witnesses in the case of the Moscow Jewish culture symposium.

## December 1976

I received a call from the deputy general director of my previous place of employment, Galakhov, on the pretext of discussing my appeal for an exit visa. There I was met by a couple of secret police (KGB) agents. One of them let me see his ID in the name Alexander Andreevich Sabirov. The other did not show any papers, and Sabirov called him Lev Nikolaevich (like the famous Russian writer Tolstoy). At that time, there was an investigation in the case of Sharansky, and they tried to intimidate me in connection with the scientific seminar at my apartment. They threatened me with arrest because participants could leak secret information to the West.

### February 1977

I was honored by another conversation with the same two KGB agents, this time at my workstation in the elevator of some apartment building where I slaved for twenty-four hours and then was off seventy-two hours. They offered me a job as a programmer in any organization of my choice, including those that did not hire me when I applied to them.

### April 1977

Yet another conversation with the same agents and at the same place. They were unhappy with me because I did not apply for any of the jobs they had offered me. I explained that I would not accept *any* gifts from them.

### April 1977

I was summoned to the Volunteer National Guard (DND in Russian) in our neighborhood. I was told that my neighbors had complained that too many people visited us and this disturbed them. I asked to see those complaints and/ or the names of the complainants. They could not do that. They simply wrote the minutes of our interview and I promised to be as civilized as I always am and was.

### April 1977

The police criminal investigation division checks the ID of my guests, participants in a scientific seminar. Two people had no ID on them, and they were dispatched to the DND.

### May 1977

The reply to my complaint to the district attorney about illegal acts by the militia stated that everything was legal because my neighbors had reported me to the militia.

## May 1977

Another routine ID check was carried out by the militia and the DND.

## June 1977

The City Prosecutor determined that the militia procedures were legal.

## August 1977

Another routine phone disconnection, this time for the third time.

## September 1977

I complained about this new disconnecting of our telephone to the district telephone office. No reply was forthcoming.

## September 1977

The City Prosecutor claimed that we violated Article 78 of the Telephone Service Regulation. It was not clear how and when.

## September 1977

Another routine ID check of our guests was carried out at our home by the DND.

## October 1977

We had yet another conversation foisted on us by the same two KGB agents at my home. This was instigated by the fact that Lev Furman and his friend were detrained from a Leningrad–Moscow Express at Bologoye Station and sent back to Leningrad. As it was on the eve of the sixtieth anniversary of the Great October Revolution, outside troublemakers were not welcome in the capital. There were more than enough local ones.

I had knowledge of this because we had train tickets for the beginning of November for a journey to Tashkent, with a stopover in Moscow. We planned to take part in a jubilee seminar for Alexander Yakovlevich Lerner (a prominent refusenik scientist).

Furman's variant was not for us; we did not keep our plans secret. I just rang (from a payphone, of course, because ours was "out of order") to Boris Granovsky and Anatoly Epstein (who is my cousin and a refusenik, too) and told them about our plans. My calculation that their phones were tapped happened to be true. In a short while, the KGB agents warned us to go wherever else we wanted, just not to Moscow. They even offered to get us airline tickets, which was a big deal then, and left their phone numbers. However, we had managed to get tickets for Tashkent without their help.

## November 1977

We received another routine refusal of our visa applications from the OVIR.

## December 16, 1977

The DND tried to prevent the American vice-consul Oscar Clyatt and his family from visiting us by pretending that there had been a theft and an investigation was being conducted). A neighbor informed us of this but requested that we not reveal our source of information. I explained to those DND fellows that the vice-consul and his family were my guests and had nothing to do with any alleged crime. They let them through.

## December 23, 1977

I was issued a summons from the district militia HQ; the subpoena stated that it was related to our complaints. Instead of dealing with my complaints, a routine conversation followed with the KGB agents. Whereas before, the threats were of a general nature, this time there was an official prohibition to meet with foreigners. Never before had I had any trouble meeting Westerners.

## December 25, 1977

We received a dinner invitation from the Clyatts at their home on Pushkin Square. The vice-consul met us met us near Pushkin Square and we marched to his place. An unknown person followed us, very clearly taking photos of us. Answering my objections, he pointed out that in our country, it is legal to take pictures in the streets. He was actually right.

## January 1978

We were stopped in the street by some tough fellow who handed us a summons to the KGB for a conversation. This time, they give me an official notification that I was banned from meeting foreigners.

## May 1978

Militiamen tried to check IDs at a juridical seminar given by Valery Segal at our apartment.

## May 1979

We continued to receive monthly visits by the *DND*. Once, a group of them demanded that I show them my documents at my home. They wanted to know whether I was employed. (By this time, I had left Repair-Building Outfit No. 4 and was employed as a secretary to a refusenik, Professor Abram Kagan). I told them that I had a job but would reveal details only to a court of law.

## April 10, 1980

Our apartment was searched. Case #49608 (13-80).

## April 14, 1980

I was interrogated at the district attorney office by Investigator E. N. Livanov.

## April 24, 1980

An attempt was made to summon me to the militia HQ.

## May 20, 1980

An article appeared in a newspaper *Vecherny Leningrad* that was called "The Business of Slander."

The original diary

Grandparents on Ida's mother's
side: Cecilia Vodovoz and
Moses Nemirovsky.
Krivoi Rog, 1898.
*From the collection
of Ida and Aba Taratuta.*

Sonya and Semion Avidon,
Ida's parents. Moscow, 1929.
*From the collection
of Ida and Aba Taratuta.*

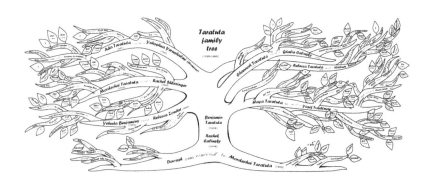

Aba's family tree
Compiled by Yael Pushkin

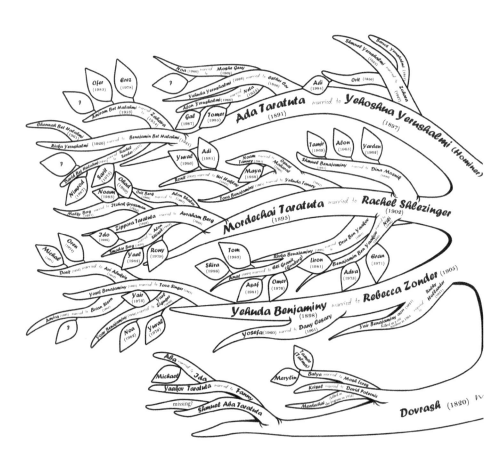

132

# Taratuta family tree

(1820-1990)

**Benjamin Taratuta**
(1852)

**Rachek Calinsky**
(1858)

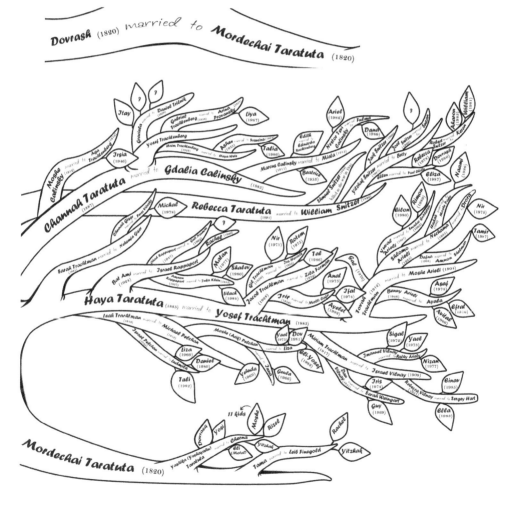

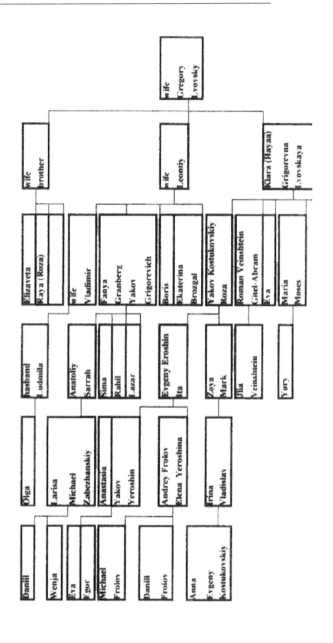

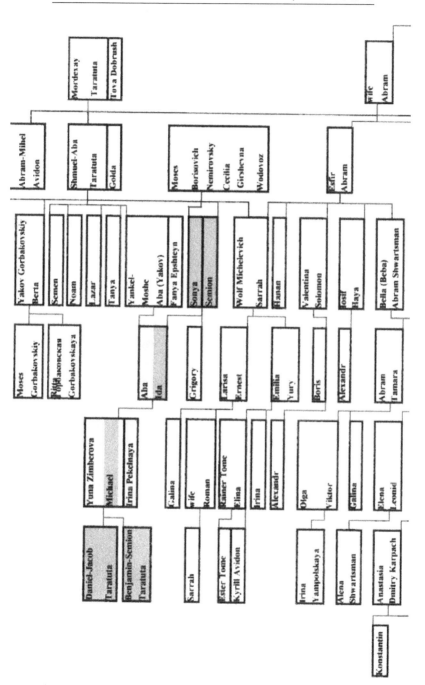

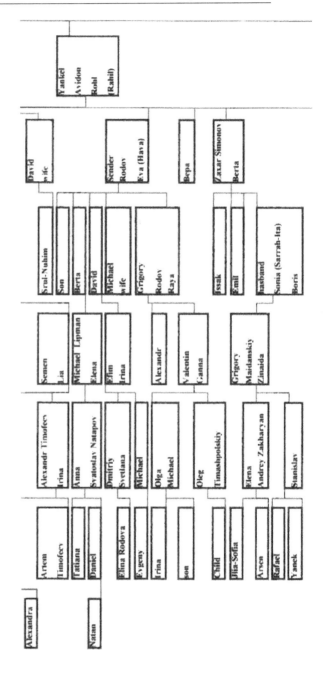

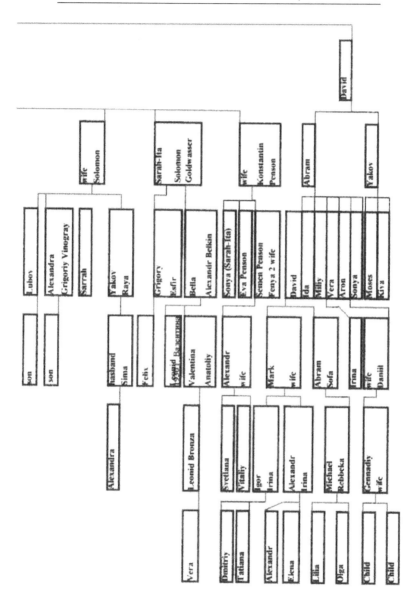

Compiled by Elena Yeroshina

Ida's grandparents from her father's side Abram-Mihel and Klara Avidon. Moscow, 1929.
*From the collection of Ida and Aba Taratuta.*

Aba's father Yaakov Taratuta.
Uman, 1925.
*From the collection
of Ida and Aba Taratuta.*

Aba's family from mother's side: Fanya Taratuta (Epstein)
Left to right: first row—Uncle Emil, mother Fanya, father Yaakov;
Second row— Uncle Isaac Epstein, Aunt Polina Epstein. Leningrad, 1965.
*From the collection of Ida and Aba Taratuta.*

Aba's family from mother's side:
Left to right: first row—grandmother Adele, great grandmother Zura-Sara Malka;
Second row: great grandfather Avraham Avrutsky, mother Fanya Taratuta (Epstein).
The middle of 1930s.
*Collection of Ida and Aba Taratuta.*

Aba's family from father's side: grandmother Golda and grandfather Shmuel-Aba Taratuta
with granddaughter Tamara Taratuta.
Leningrad, 1925.
*From the collection of Ida and Aba Taratuta.*

Ida's and Aba's wedding. Leningrad, 1960.
*From the collection of Ida and Aba Taratuta.*

Ida with one-year-old Misha, Leningrad, 1961.
*From the collection of Ida and Aba Taratuta.*

Misha in the army, 1982.
*From the collection
of Ida and Aba Taratuta.*

Exhibition of Misha Taratuta's works USA, 1988.
*Collection of Ida and Aba Taratuta.*

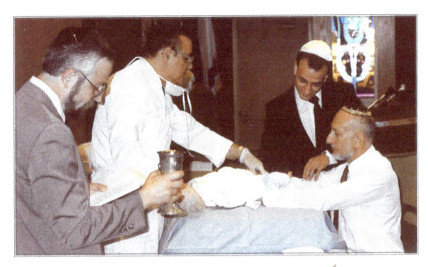

Circumcision (brit milah) of our first grandchild Daniel.
Aba Taratuta holds grandson, Misha standing by. USA, 1991.
*From the collection of Ida and Aba Taratuta.*

Misha with his children: Daniel and Benjamin. USA, 1995.
*From the collection of Ida and Aba Taratuta.*

With Aba's relatives from mother's side.
Left to right: first row—Shuric and Alla Groisman, Misha Taratuta and Irina Pecelny;
second row—Natasha, Clara and Anatoly Epstein, Luba and Sasha Epstein, Aba,
Yuri Epstein; third row—Tanya and Mark Epstein, Ida Taratuta. Israel, 2000.
*From the collection of Ida and Aba Taratuta.*

With Benjamin Khaikin—our first Hebrew teacher.
From left: Asna and Benjamin Khaikin, Ida and Aba Taratuta. Leningrad, 1974.
*From the collection of Ida and Aba Taratuta.*

Boris Granovsky teaches Hebrew. Leningrad, 1977.
*From the collection of Ida and Aba Taratuta.*

A group of activists from Leningrad.
From left: Aba, Lilya Shapiro, Ida Taratuta, behind her—Lev Shapiro
and Yuri Shpeizman. Remember and Save Association.
*From the collection of Nelly Lipovich-Shpeizman.*

A group of Leningrad veteran Refusniks.    From left to right:
Alexander Chertin;  (not known);  Alexander Lunts; ' Aba Taratuta
(waiting since May 1973);   Viktor Savitsky (end of 1973);
Leonid Lotvin (recently emigrated);  and Evgeny Abezgaus (September 1973).

From page of the weekly bulletin "Jews in the U.S.S.R." published in London (May 30, 1975) with the photo of group of Leningrad activists during their demonstration in Moscow. From left: Alexander Chertin, Valentin Stanislavsky, Alexander Lunts (Moscow), Aba Taratuta, Victor Savitsky, Leonid Lotvin, Eugene Abeshaus. December 1974 . Remember and Save Association.

*From the Nan Greifer, Jews in the USSR (England).*

Scientific seminar in the apartment of the Taratuta family. From left to right: Aba, Eugene Borukhovich, Michael Nosovsky. Leningrad, 1977.
*From the collection of Ida and Aba Taratuta.*

Boris Kalendarev, who was convicted for refusing to serve in the army. In the camp in Elista, Kalmykia, 1980. Remember and Save Association. *From the collection of Kalendarev family.*

The group of Jewish artists "Aleph".
From left: Alexander Manusov, Boris Rabinovich, Yuri Kalendarev,
Alec Rapoport, Sima Ostrovsky, sitting—Eugene Abeshaus. Leningrad, 1975.
Remember and Save Association.
*From the collection Natasha and Eugene Abeshaus.*

With Galina and Alec Zelichonok.
Israel, 1995.
*From the collection of Ida and Aba Taratuta.*

With Isaak Furshtein, who owned
the collection of Jewish books,
used by the Jews of Leningrad.
Cleveland, USA, 1988.
*From the collection of Ida and Aba Taratuta.*

A group of activists from Leningrad. From left: first row—Luda Varnavitsky,
Natasha Harmats-Abeshaus, Olga Chertin; second row—Irma Chernyak,
Alexander Boguslavsky, Leonid Reinis, Ida and Aba Taratuta,
Eugene Abeshaus. Leningrad, 1975.
*From the collection of Ida and Aba Taratuta.*

Tamara Brill and Jean Gaffin (England)—our first foreign guests after receiving refusal to repatriate to Israel. Leningrad, 1973 Remember and Save Association.
*From the collection of Tamara Brill.*

Shirley Goldstein (Omaha, Nebraska, USA) visits Taratuta's family. From left: Ida, Misha, Shirley, Aba. Leningrad, December 1973. Remember and Save Association.
*From the collection of Shirley Goldstein.*

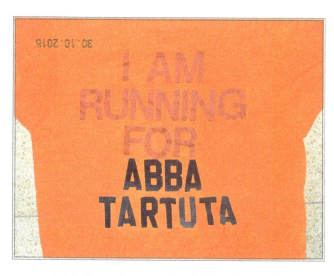

T Shirt from a demonstration for Soviet Jews, USA.
The end of the 1970s.  Remember and Save Association.
*From the collection of Shirley Goldstein.*

The visit of Marike Romer,
Finland.
From left: Aba, Marike,
Ida Taratuta, Vera Sheiba.
Leningrad, beginning
of the 1980s.
*From the collection
of Ida and Aba Taratuta.*

British historian Sir Martin Gilbert (right) visits Ida and Aba Taratuta.
Leningrad, 1984.
*From the collection of Michael Beizer.*

Aba with Enid Wurtman, veteran of movement
for Soviet Jews from the 1970's. From Philadelphia; lives
in Jerusalem. Israel 2008. Remember and Save Association.
*From the collection of Enid Wurtman.*

US Vice Consul in Leningrad Daniel Grossman (center)
in Ida and Aba's apartment. Leningrad, 1985.
*From the collection of Ida and Aba Taratuta.*

With the producer of the documentary film "Refusenik," Laura Bialis. From left:
Avi Vaknin (Laura's husband), Laura, Moscow activist Yuli Kosharovsky, Aba.
Israel, 2008. Remember and Save Association.
*From the Enid Wutrman Collection.*

Demonstration of refuseniks near the Leningrad party headquarters (former Smolny
Institute). From left: Michael Beizer (with poster), Aba and Ida Taratuta,
Boris Lokshin, Lilya Shapiro, Inna Rozhansky-Lobovikov, Lena Keis-Kuna.
Leningrad, March 23, 1987. Remember and Save Association.
*Photo by Alexander Frankel.*

Demonstration of refuseniks near the Leningrad party headquarter.
From left: Tanya Makushkina, Stanislav Mezhibovsky, Misha, Ida and Aba Taratuta,
Inna Rozhansky-Lobovikov, Lena Keis-Kuna, Lilya Shapiro, Vladimir Knoch, Rimma
Sosna, Boris Lokshin, Mark Budnyatsky. Leningrad, April 1987.
Remember and Save Association.
*From the collection of Vladimir Lifshitz.*

Demonstration of refuseniks on Isaac's Square.
From leftt: Alexander Yampolsky, Lev Furman, Leonid Kelbert, Nikita Demin (Avrum Shmulevich), Vladimir Lifshitz, Michael and Tanya Makushkin, Boris Lifshitz, Mark Budnyatsky, Rimma Sosna, Aba Taratuta, Inna Rozhansky-Lobovikov, Boris Dubrov, Boris Lokshin. Leningrad, June 1987. Remember and Save Association.
*From the collection of Ida and Aba Taratuta.*

Andrei Leshchinsky and Natan Rodzin looking at the house built by them, together with Aba and other refuseniks, in the village Siverskaya in the 1980s. Leningrad region, 2015. Remember and Save Association.
*From the collection of Nathan Rodzin.*

A group of skiers in the Russian bath during Aba's visit to Leningrad in 1992. From left: Leonid Sorokopud, Alexander Malkov, Volodya Panchenko, Yasha Herman, Aba.
*From the collection of Ida and Aba Taratuta.*

At a ski resort. From left: Abram Kagan, Volodya Panchenko, Ilya Simovsky, Misha and
Aba Taratuta. Kirovsk, North Russia, the beginning of the 1980s.
*From the collection of Ida and Aba Taratuta.*

Meeting at the Moscow station with Prisoner of Zion Vladimir Lifshitz on his return
from prison. From left: Anya Lifshitz, Aba Taratuta, Alec Zelichonok, Vladimir
Lifshitz, Boris Devyatov. Leningrad, 1987. Remember and Save Association.
*From the collection of Vladimir Lifshitz.*

**154**

Ida and Aba Taratuta leave their friends to go to Israel at last, after 15 years in refusal.
From left: Fanya Taratuta, Vladimir Berlin, Vera Sheiba, Ida Taratuta, Natan Rodzin,
Mila Kovshilovsky, Sasha Avrutsky, Aba Taratuta.
Pulkovo Airport, Leningrad, January 3, 1988.
*From the collection of Ida and Aba Taratuta.*

Presentations at the annual dinner hosted by Lynn Singer to collect donations
for the struggle for Soviet Jewry. From left: Lynn Singer, Ida and Aba Taratuta,
Masha and Volodya Slepak. New York, March 1988.
Remember and Save Association.
*From the collection of Lynn Singer.*

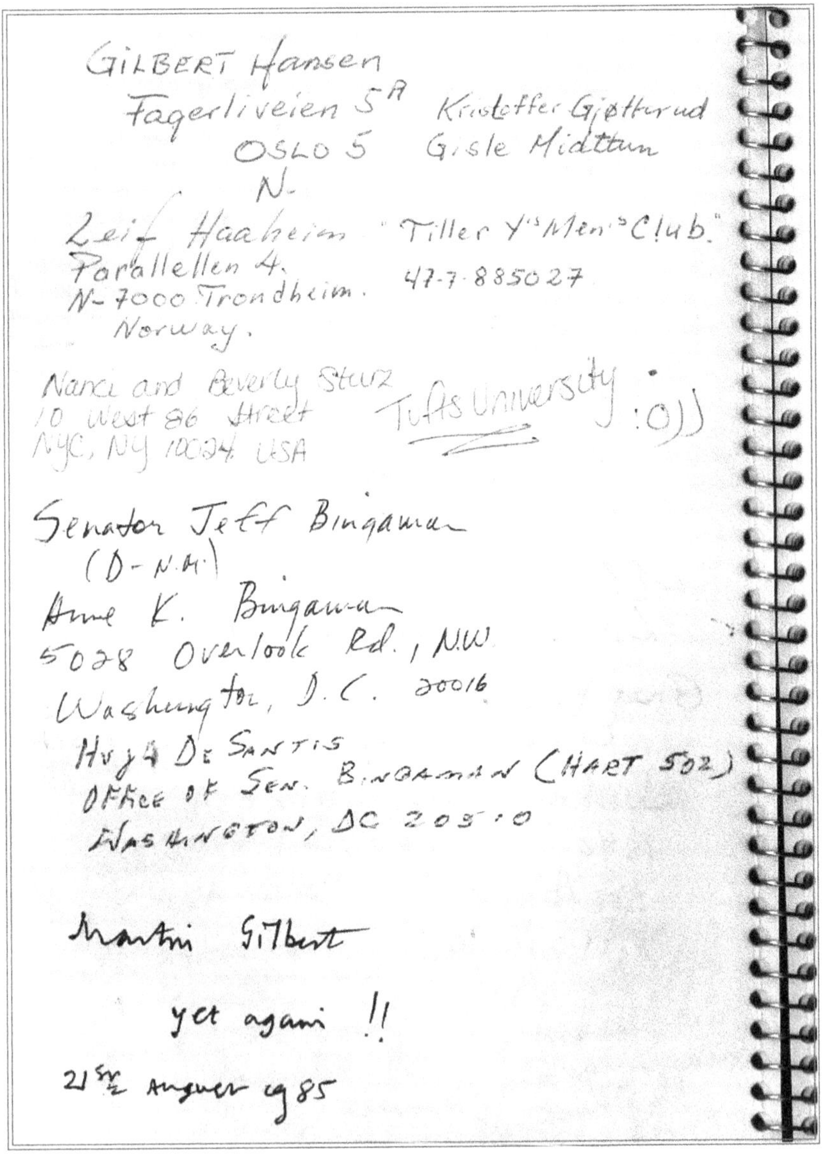

GILBERT Hansen
Fagerliveien 5^A   Kristoffer Gjøtterud
OSLO 5   Gisle Midttun
N.
Leif Haaheim   "Tiller Y'Men' Club."
Parallellen 4.      47-7-885027
N-7000 Trondheim.
Norway.

Nanci and Beverly Sturz   Tufts University
10 West 86 Street                                :0))
NYC, NY 10024 USA

Senator Jeff Bingaman
(D-N.M.)
Anne K. Bingaman
5028 Overlook Rd., N.W.
Washington, D.C. 20016
Hugh De Santis
Office of Sen. Bingaman (HART 502)
Washington, DC 20510

Martin Gilbert

yet again !!
21st August 1985

A page from the Taratuta's Guest Book with records, business cards and names
of foreign visitors.Leningrad, 1980-1987.
*From the collection of Ida and Aba Taratuta*

Our visit to Bunny and Frank Brodsky. From left: Marvin Verman,
Frank and Bunny, Ida Taratuta. Philadelphia, 1988.
*From the collection of Ida and Aba Taratuta.*

Meeting with British veteran of the movement for Soviet Jewry, Michael Sherbourne.
From left: top row—Michael, Shirley Goldstein, Aba, Leonid Ratner; bottom row—
Muriel Sherbourne, Michael's wife, Julie Ratner. Israel, the beginning of the 1990s.
*From the collection of Ida and Aba Taratuta.*

The board members of the Remember and Save Association. From left: Michael Beizer, Aba, Shmuel Kessler, Edward Markov. Haifa, 2014. Remember and Save Association.
*From the Edward Markov Collection.*

Opening of the exhibition "Jews of Struggle", dedicated to the fortieth anniversary of the Jewish movement in the Soviet Union's repatriation to Israel. Speaker Aba Taratuta. Diaspora Museum, Tel Aviv, 2007. Remember and Save Association.
*Diaspora Museum Foundation.*

# Index

CPSIA information can be obtained
at www.ICGtesting.com
Printed in the USA
BVHW011943061019
560346BV00004B/83/P